"Sarah's knowledge and enthusiasm for discovering a woman's true beauty is bar none! Whether you are a fashion guru or a fashion victim, she will take you from flawed to fabulous! This book is a road map to the styles and clothes that flatter YOUR body."

— **Cibeline Sariano,** Fashion Designer/Boutique Owner, www.cibelinesariano.com

DRESS YOURSELF *Skinny**

Dressing The Body You Have
To Look Like The Body You Want

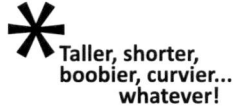

*Taller, shorter, boobier, curvier... whatever!

Sarah Shah

Fideli Publishing
www.fidelipublishing.com

Dress Yourself Skinny

Sarah Shah

Published by:
Fideli Publishing

ISBN: 978-1-60414-251-8

Publisher's Cataloging-in-Publication
(Provided by Quality Books, Inc.)

Shah, Sarah.
    Dress yourself skinny : dressing the body you have to look like the body you want / Sarah Shah.
    p. cm.
    Includes index.
    ISBN-13: 978-1-60414-251-8
    ISBN-10: 1-60414-251-0

    1. Women's clothing. 2. Body image in women.
I. Title.

GT1720.S53 2010   391'.2
                         QBI10-600061

Dedication

Thank you to my clients for inspiring this book.
Our work together has refined and
proven these strategies.
This book wouldn't have
been possible without you!

Thank you Wasabi, Mattison and Lisa for
believing in me every step of the way.

Acknowledgements

Thank you to the great team that brought this project to life!

Mattison Grey, Business Coach,
MattisonGrey.com

Wendy Bowser, Editor

Myrna Galan, Graphic Designer
GalanGraphix.com

Katie Dylewski, Illustrator

Robin Surface, Publisher
Fideli Publishing.com

Dan Poynter, ParaPublishing.com

CONTENTS

PREFACE

Contrary to current myth, image isn't everything. The person you are on the inside is most important. Women of all sizes and shapes, however, have developed the habit of judging their bodies harshly and finding faults that others wouldn't – and don't – even notice. Over time, this negative self-talk wears down your self-esteem and injures your spirit.

This book is designed to help you recognize the beautiful person you are on the outside and honor the exquisite being you are on the inside. You'll find strategies to make the most of your figure and diagrams of the perfect clothing styles for you.

Flattering your body has nothing to do with the amount of money you spend. Want proof? Just look at the society pages in your local newspaper for examples of some women who look frumpy and lumpy in expensive, designer clothing. There are figure-flattering choices whether you shop at a discount store or the priciest, most exclusive boutiques.

As you begin reading this book, I invite you to take a picture of yourself in your current look to record your starting point. Come back to this photo as you step through your transformation so you can appreciate your progress.

The companion Dress Yourself Skinny workbook will provide further support as you transform your wardrobe and document the emergence of your new body.

CHAPTER 1
You Have A Beautiful Body

H uman beings are just like precious stones. We have flaws. These flaws go virtually unnoticed when we are masterfully cut and polished. Unfortunately, most women have developed dressing habits that obscure the facets of their beauty rather than enhancing them.

In the quest for comfortable clothing, it's easy to settle for styles that aren't flattering or fashionable. In the effort to camouflage our imperfections, we often cover up our best qualities. For example, have you ever worn an oversized shirt or jacket to try to cover up a lump or roll? The boxy jacket does cover the roll, and it also adds volume to your body making you look 10, 20 or even 30 pounds heavier than you are. There is a better way!

Most of us learned rigid fashion rules in our teens and twenties. At the time, those old beauty rules were the best that fashion had to offer. The continuing evolution of technology, fabrics and color allows us to create new styles, foundations and combinations that we couldn't even imagine just 10 years ago.

The new rules offer more ways to flatter women's bodies. This book will show you how to choose garments that are perfect for you. The right choices will balance your proportions visually and literally change your body before your eyes. You can have everything you want – clothing that feels good and makes you look great!

In these pages, you'll find ways to feel great about the body you have today. These strategies also can supercharge a weight-loss program by letting you see results faster and give you inspiration to get to your target size.

And for those of you who would like to appear taller, shorter, curvier, leaner or even heavier, there are solutions for you, too. It's time to uncover that full-length mirror and make it your new best friend!

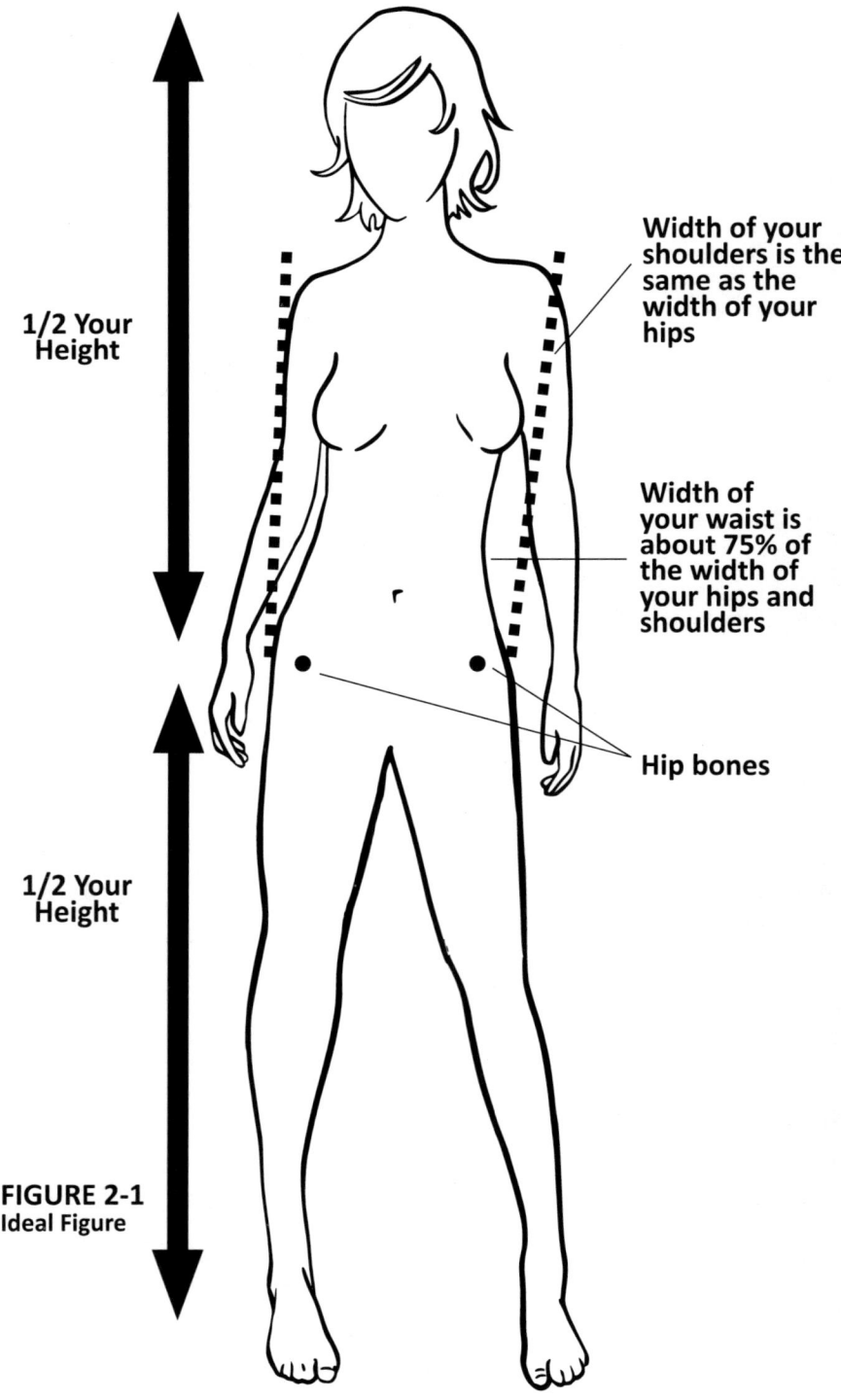

1/2 Your Height

Width of your shoulders is the same as the width of your hips

Width of your waist is about 75% of the width of your hips and shoulders

Hip bones

1/2 Your Height

FIGURE 2-1
Ideal Figure

CHAPTER 2

Essentials Of A "Skinny" Body

Society's definition of the "ideal" woman's body is an hourglass shape with the shoulders and hips about the same width; breasts within the rib cage and nipples lifted to a level between the elbow and shoulder; waist that is about the height of your bent elbow and about 3/4 the width of your hips and shoulders; and the distance from the top of your head to hipbones is the same as the distance from the hipbones to your toes (Figure 2-1).

Most of us don't have these proportions, but we can fake it with our clothing choices. There are some general strategies that flatter almost everyone. The four steps to revealing your beautiful body within are:

Step 1   Smooth Operator: Eliminate lumps, bumps and rolls.

Step 2   Size Doesn't Matter: Ignore the tag.

Step 3   Go Vertical: Look taller to appear thinner (skip this section if you're tall).

Step 4   Master The Art Of Illusion (skip this section if you're tall).

There also are some specific suggestions and style choices to flatter your particular body type.

Step 5   Determine Your Body Type.

Step 6   Just get M.A.D. about your new look!
           Maximize or minimize your area of concern,
           Adjust the proportions to create your hourglass figure, and
           Distract attention to your assets.

Details about these steps are provided in the following chapters.

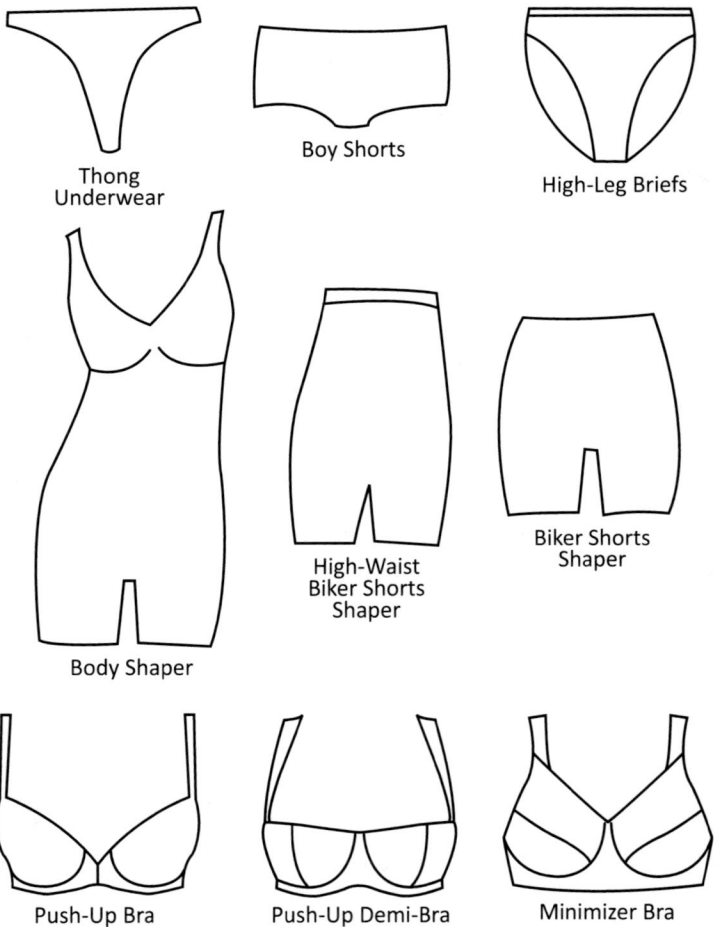

Thong
Underwear

Boy Shorts

High-Leg Briefs

Body Shaper

High-Waist
Biker Shorts
Shaper

Biker Shorts
Shaper

Push-Up Bra

Push-Up Demi-Bra

Minimizer Bra

CHAPTER 3

Smooth Operator: Eliminating Lumps, Bumps & Rolls

Some underwear, body shapers and pantyhose squeeze out more than they smooth out. Often, they actually create bumps and bulges that you don't really have. The wrong underwear and foundation garments can create back-boobs, tummy rolls, muffin-tops, visible panty lines (VPLs) and other random bulges. These bumps and bulges make you look heavier and more out of shape than you really are.

Here are some tips for choosing the right underwear:

a. Underwear that lies flat against the body keeps you looking smooth. Choose underwear with smooth edges and without tight elastic, seams or bands that squeeze you at the edge. Thongs, boy shorts and high-leg briefs are good choices for most bodies.

If you have a tummy, choose styles that cover the belly so it doesn't hang over the top. Hanky Panky makes thongs and boy shorts that lie perfectly flat on the body. Soma Intimates Vanishing Edge High Leg Brief is a full coverage panty that virtually erases panty lines.

b. If you wear "shape wear" (modern girdles), opt for smoothers instead of shapers. They have lighter control so they smooth rather than squeeze. If you want to smooth the waist area or tummy area, choose the full body shaper or high-waist bike shorts that extend from the bottom bra band to mid-thigh. This style will smooth the entire torso without creating VPLs or the dreaded bulges at the waist.

If you want to smooth just the hips and bottom, opt for the regular, bike-shorts shaper.

Shapers made by Body Wrap (about $80, in department stores and specialty boutiques) and No Nonsense (about $4, in drug stores and supermarkets) are good options.

c. The right bra will virtually eliminate back and underarm bulges. Help from a bra professional is the only way to get a bra that really fits. Bra fitting is more art than a science. Variances in brands, styles, materials and fabrication will affect the way a bra fits. Beware of the bra fitter who uses a measuring tape. The best fitters use their instincts and experience to find the right bra.

d. Often, a great fitting bra will introduce you to new letters of the alphabet. You may think you are a B, C or D and find out that you really are a AA, DD, E, F... etc.

e. Here are some bra fit tips (see Figures 3-1 and 3-2):

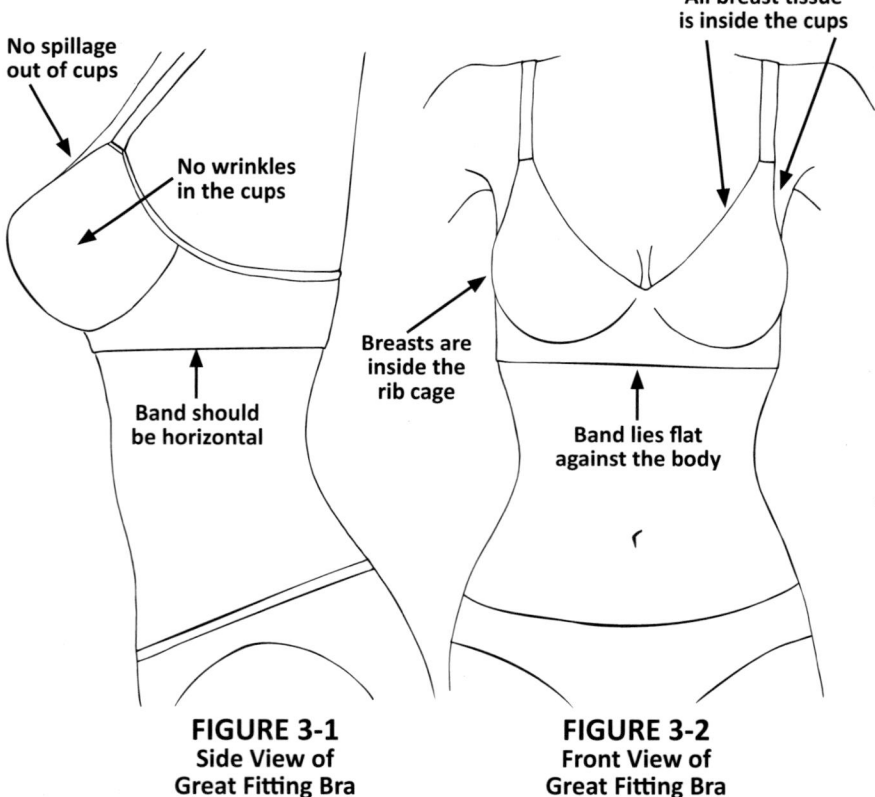

FIGURE 3-1
Side View of
Great Fitting Bra

FIGURE 3-2
Front View of
Great Fitting Bra

THE CUPS

• Your breasts should sit perfectly within the cups. To get the best results, lean over at the waist with your bra on and let your breast tissue hang "free." Lift the tissue with your hand and place it into the cup and return to a standing position.

- Except for push-up styles, the cup
  no breast tissue should poke out the
  should lay around your breasts, agai

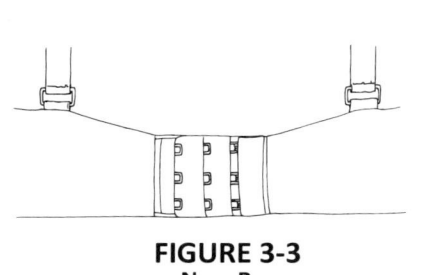

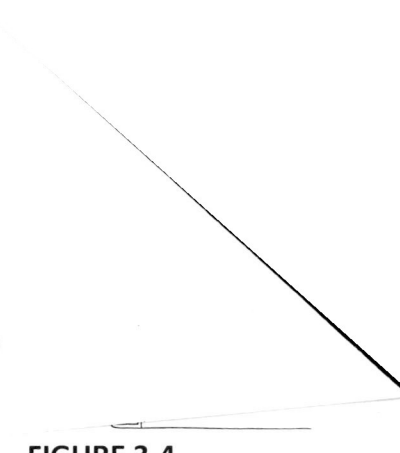

DRESS YOURSELF SKINNY

FIGURE 3-3
New Bra

FIGURE 3-4
Old Bra

THE BAND

- The bra band should be level with the floor around your whole body.

- The band should be snug around your ribcage so it doesn't move up or down when you move.

- The front of the bra band should sit flat against your body, especially when raising your arms.

- The front of the bra band should sit directly under the breast tissue.

- Most people don't realize that most of the bra's support comes from the band. The straps are used to bring the cups closer to your body.

- Bras stretch over time. When you first buy a bra, choose one that fits with the band on the biggest clasps (Figure 3-3). As the bra ages, close the bra band on the smaller clasps to counteract the stretching and maintain a good fit (figure 3-4).

f. For more bra fitting advice, check out the Boobologist at www.ShopIsabella.com.

FIGURE 4-1
Clothing That
Fits Too Loosely

FIGURE 4-2
Clothing That
Fits Too Tightly

FIGURE 4-3
Clothing That
Fits Just Right

CHAPTER 4

Size Doesn't Matter: Ignore The Tag

Sizing standards are an illusion. The actual size of sizes can vary dramatically by brands, fabrics and styles. A size can be bigger or smaller than you assume it is.

The most important element of a great looking body is great fitting clothes. Ignore the size on the tag so you can find clothing that fits really well. If you don't like the number the manufacturer has assigned, when you get your new clothing home, use a Sharpie to cross out the size and write in any number you like!

Keep in mind the following:

- Clothing that is too loose makes you look juvenile, like a little girl dressing up in her mother's slip and high heels (Figure 4-1). Clothing that is too big makes you appear to be too small.

- Clothing that is too small and tight makes you look like you are bursting out of your clothes, like the Incredible Hulk (Figure 4-2). Clothing that is too small actually makes you look too big.

- Clothing that is just right skims the body without pulling or gaping. Clothing that fits well makes your body look leaner and slimmer (Figure 4-3).

CHAPTER 5

Go Vertical: How To Look Taller*
*If you are taller than you want to be, skip to Chapter 7

Looking taller makes you look thinner. Here are some ways to add to your height. Choose and combine any or all of the following:

- Reveal your throat and chest with scoop and "V" necklines.

- Choose fabrics with vertical or diagonal stripes. Anything from subtle pin stripes to wide bold stripes will work.

- Choose pieces with built-in vertical lines, such as princess seams, fringe details or corduroy fabric.

- Create vertical lines by tying long, thin scarves around the neck or waist or wearing long jewelry, such as pendants, lariat necklaces or even dangling earrings.

- All deep colors are slimming. You aren't limited to wearing all black. Create a monochromatic or monotone look by wearing tops and bottoms in the same color, intensity or shade. Experiment with colors like burgundy, navy, charcoal, gray, brown, green or purple. Mix them up or just wear one color from head to toe.

- Create vertical hairstyles, such as up-dos, high ponytails, half-up, half-down styles or straight hairstyle. Your hairstylist will be able to guide you.

- Lengthen pants so the hems are about 1-inch above the floor behind your heel.

- Wear shoes with heels or platform soles, even ½-inch makes a difference. Also look for shoes with a low vamp (the upper part of the shoe).

Some examples of these styles are provided in the diagrams on the following pages.

TOPS:

Scoop Neckline

V-Neckline

Diagonal Stripes

Vertical Pin Stipes

Create Multiple "V's"

Princess Seams

Vertical Fringe Details

HAIRSTYLES:

Up-Do Hairstyle

Bob Hairstyle

Half-Up, Half-Down Hairstyle

High Ponytail

Long Hairstyle

ACCESSORIES:

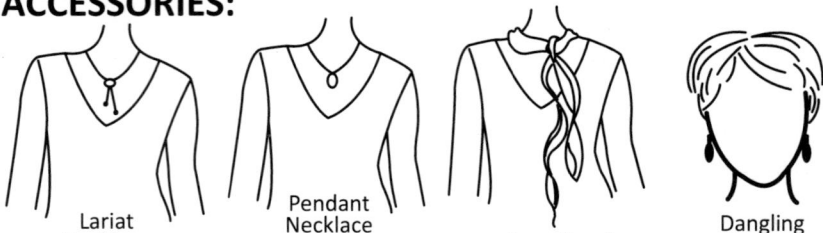

Lariat Necklace

Pendant Necklace

Long Scarf

Dangling Earrings

SHOES:

Kitten Heel Mule

Wedge Heel
Flip Flop

Platform Pump

Knee Boot

Open-Toe Pump

Pump

Slingback Sandal

Open-Toe
Wedge Heel

High Heel
Mule

Open-Toe Platform
Slingback

Wedge Heel
Mule

Closed-Toe
Slingback

Closed-Toe
Mule

CHAPTER 6

Master The Art of Illusion*
*If you are taller than you want to be, skip to Chapter 7

Clothing can either flatter or distort your body. Here are some do's and don'ts for choosing clothing that is universally flattering.

THE DO'S
These items will make you look taller and leaner. Choose and mix any of the following:

- A bra that fits perfectly is worth its weight in gold. It miraculously makes your waist smaller. To get a bra that fits properly, you have to try them on in the store. It really helps to have professional assistance. Check out Chapter 3 for bra fitting tips.

- Choose underwear with invisible edges that fits smoothly on your body and doesn't create any visible bulges or lines.

- Choose clothing that floats smoothly along your body. It should be fitted enough to show your shape and loose enough so it doesn't pull, gape, grab onto a bulge or squeeze anything out the top or sides.

- Opt for tops and jackets with hems that fall about three inches below your hipbones. This is long enough to cover most of the tummy. Any longer and your hips and bottom will look bigger than they are.

- Choose A-line skirts to skim over your bottom and hips. The most flattering hem lengths fall between the top of the knee and about two inches below the knee.

- Choose flat-waist pants, those styles with a flat waistband without any pleating, elastic, gathers, belt loops or pockets in the waist or hips. This style will make the tummy appear flatter and the hips appear smoother.

- Select trouser or boot-cut style pants with the waistband just below your natural waist.

- Hem pants about 1-inch above the floor at the back of your heel with your shoes on. You may want to have different pants for flats and high-heels shoes.

- With skirts, wearing shoes that are the same tone as your skin is slimming. For a lean look, pantyhose should be the same color as your skin and opaque tights should be the same color as your shoes.

- When selecting cover-ups and sexy robes, be sure to choose fabrics that are transparent or translucent (i.e. organza, chiffon, eyelet, mesh) so your silhouette is visible through the garment. If you choose an opaque fabric for these garments, you'll add too much bulk to your figure, making you look heavier.

TOPS:

BOTTOMS:

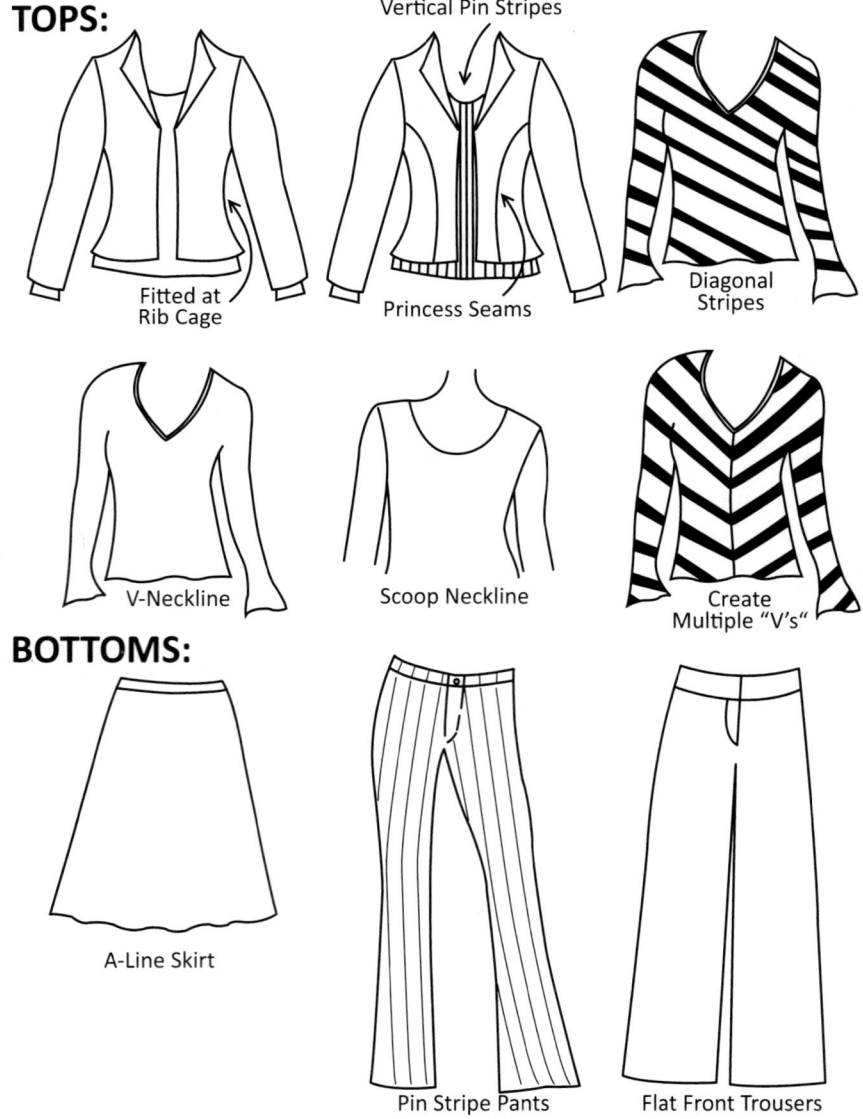

Vertical Pin Stripes

Fitted at Rib Cage

Princess Seams

Diagonal Stripes

V-Neckline

Scoop Neckline

Create Multiple "V's"

A-Line Skirt

Pin Stripe Pants

Flat Front Trousers

Boot Cut Pants   Pants with Standard Size Back Pockets

HAIRSTYLES:

High Ponytail

Bob Hairstyle

Up-Do Hairstyle

Half-Up, Half-Down Hairstyle

Long Hairstyle

ACCESSORIES:

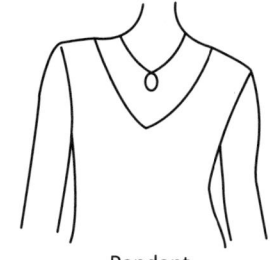

Pendant Necklace

Handbag

Clutch

Dangling Earrings

ACCESSORIES:

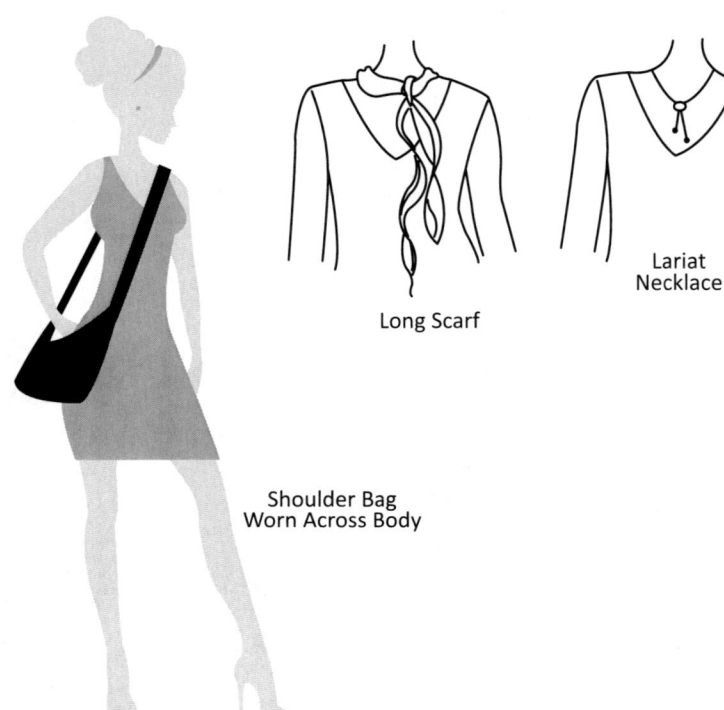

Lariat
Necklace

Long Scarf

Shoulder Bag
Worn Across Body

SHOES:

Open-Toe Pump

Pump

Open-Toe
Wedge

Closed-Toe
Mule

Wedge Heel
Mule

Open-Toe
Platform Slingback

Platform
Pump

High Heel
Mule

Closed-Toe
Slingback

Slingback
Sandal

Kitten Heel
Mule

Wedge Heel
Flip Flop

Flat Shoe

Knee Boot

THE DON'TS
These items will make you look shorter and wider. Avoid the following:

- Boxy, loose or oversized clothing may make you feel like you're hiding your flaws and imperfections. In reality, they make you look bigger by adding bulk and volume to your frame and hiding the hourglass.

- Avoid tops, jackets and sweaters that are longer than three inches below your hipbones. You might feel like longer tops will hide your bottom and hips. However, these styles actually make your hips and bottom look wider.

- Skip anything with a horizontal element or detail such as thin or bold horizontal stripes, horizontal patterns, cuffs or contrasting belts. These details make you look thicker and shorter.

- Pants with pleated waists or hips are supposed to camouflage the tummy area. Actually, this style adds bulk to the hips and tummy and makes these areas look bigger.

- Pants that are tapered at the ankles (i.e. "Mom Jeans") make your hips appear to be the widest part of your body. This style of pants turns an hourglass figure into a diamond shape, with the widest part across your hips and bottom. In this case, a diamond is NOT a girl's best friend. Yes, those pants do make your butt look big!

- Pants with side-seam pockets or back pockets with flaps make your hips and bottom look wider.

- "Skinny jeans," leggings and bike shorts fit tightly across the hips, butt, thighs and calves. These styles also make the hips and bottom the widest part of the body and make EVERYONE'S butt look big.

- Skirts with hems longer than two inches below the knee make you appear shorter and wider.

- Shoes with ankle straps and gladiator styles cross your leg at the ankle and make your legs look shorter and wider, along with the rest of your body.

TOPS:

Bow-Tie Blouse

Boxy Jacket

Gathered & Blousey Top

Jewel Neckline

Horizontal Stripes

Batwing Sleeve
(Sleeve begins at waist)

Double Breasted Jacket

Horizontal Stripes

Long Blazer

BOTTOMS:

Long Skirt

Capri Pants

Bike Shorts

Pants with Side Seam Pockets

Pants with Small Back Pockets

Pleated High-Waisted Pants

High-Waisted Tapered Jeans

Cigarette/ Skinny Pants

Pants with Cuffs

Leggings

Pants with Flap Back Pockets

DRESSES:

Dress with Yoke & Bow

Trapeze Dress

Voluminous Drapey Dress

HAIRSTYLES:

Flip
Hairstyle

ACCESSORIES:

Stud Earrings

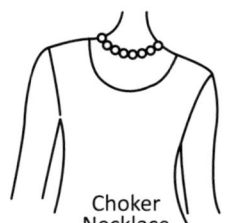

Choker
Necklace

Short Scarf

SHOES:

High Heal with
Ankle Strap

Slouchy Boot

Chunky
Heel Shoe

Gladiator
Sandal

High Front
Mule

High Front
Slingback

Ankle Boot

So now what? You can apply these new rules in Chapters 3 thru 6 to your existing clothes or take a shopping trip and create the new you. When you work with your current wardrobe, separate the clothes that work from the ones that don't. A tailor may be able to breathe new life into some of the pieces that don't work.

Purge the clothes that don't work so you aren't tempted to keep wearing them. Wearing a few clothes that look great is better than wearing lots of clothes that don't. You are too hot to settle!

Try the ideas in Steps 1 thru 4 and see what happens. You'll be surprised by how good you look! Compare your new look to your "before" picture and see what's different.

If you're ready for more, the following chapters provide specific suggestions and clothing recommendations based on your body characteristics.

CHAPTER 7
Find Your Body Type

No matter how perfectly others see you, most wor with their bodies. The first step to improving you~ ⌐ identify your body type. This chapter outlines each of the common ~~ types. Sketches also are included to help you recognize the characteristics of each figure.

Which body type is most like yours? If you're not sure, here's an easy way to figure it out.

1. Get two rolls of inexpensive wrapping paper or kraft paper (at least 6 feet long and 2½ feet wide) and unroll them on the floor.

2. Lay the two sheets next to each other, matching up the long edges, so you have a sheet that's about 5 feet wide and 6 feet long.

3. Lie down on the paper in your underwear. Keep your arms straight at your sides without touching your torso or hips. Keep your legs straight and together, but not touching and your toes unpointed.

4. Have a friend draw the outline of your body with a marker as close to your body as possible and without drawing on your skin.

5. To find your hipbones, place your hands on your hips. With your index fingers, feel the curve of your pelvic bones. The part of your pelvic bone that is closest to the center of your body is the "hipbone" (see Figure 2-1 on page 2).

Identify your body type(s) by comparing your dimensions on the paper to the descriptions of each of the following sketches of the different body types (width of shoulders, waist and hips and length from head to hipbones and from hipbones to heels).

- **Big Breasts** – Bust is wider than hips and shoulders or bigger than you want them to be (Figure 7-2).

- **Small Breasts** – Bust is narrower than hips and shoulders or smaller than you want them to be (Figure 7-3).

- **Wide Shoulders** – Shoulders are wider than hips or wider than you want them to be (Figure 7-4).

- **Narrow Shoulders** – Shoulders are more narrow than hips or more narrow than you want them to be (Figure 7-5).

- **Tummy or Thick Waist** – Waist is wider than ¾ of the width of hips and shoulders or tummy protrudes from the torso further than you'd like (Figure 7-6).

- **Short Waist or Short Torso** – Your bent elbow is below your waist and the distance from the top of your head to your hipbones is shorter than the distance from your hipbones to the floor (Figure 7-7).

- **Long Waist or Long Torso** – Your bent elbow is above your waist and the distance from the top of your head to your hipbones is longer than the distance from your hipbones to the floor (Figure 7-8).

- **Wide Hips** – Your bottom or hips are wider than your shoulders or wider than you'd like (Figure 7-9).

- **Narrow Hips** – Your hips are more narrow than your shoulders or narrower than you'd like (Figure 7-10).

- **Tall** – You are taller than you want to be (Figure 7-11).

- **Short** – You are shorter than you want to be (Figure 7-12).

- **Straight Figure** – The width of your bust, waist and hips is about the same or you are less curvy than you'd like to be (Figure 7-13).

- **Skinny** – You are skinnier than you want to be (Figure 7-14).

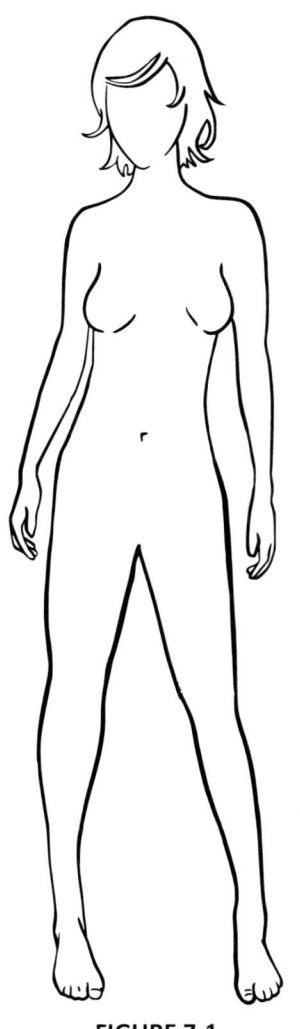 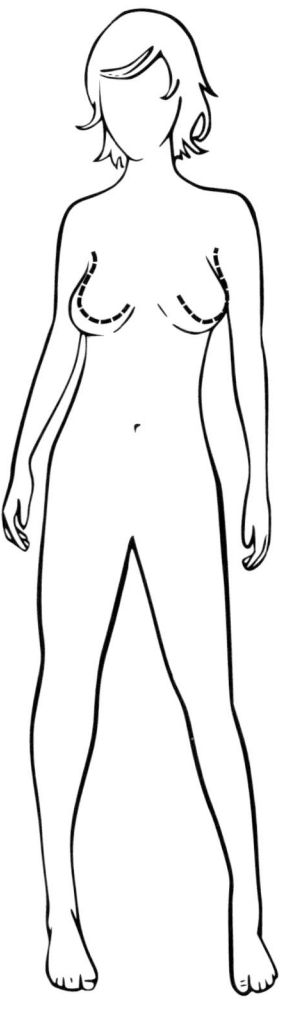

FIGURE 7-1
Ideal Figure

FIGURE 7-2
Big Breasts – Bust is
wider than hips and
shoulders or bigger than
you want them to be.

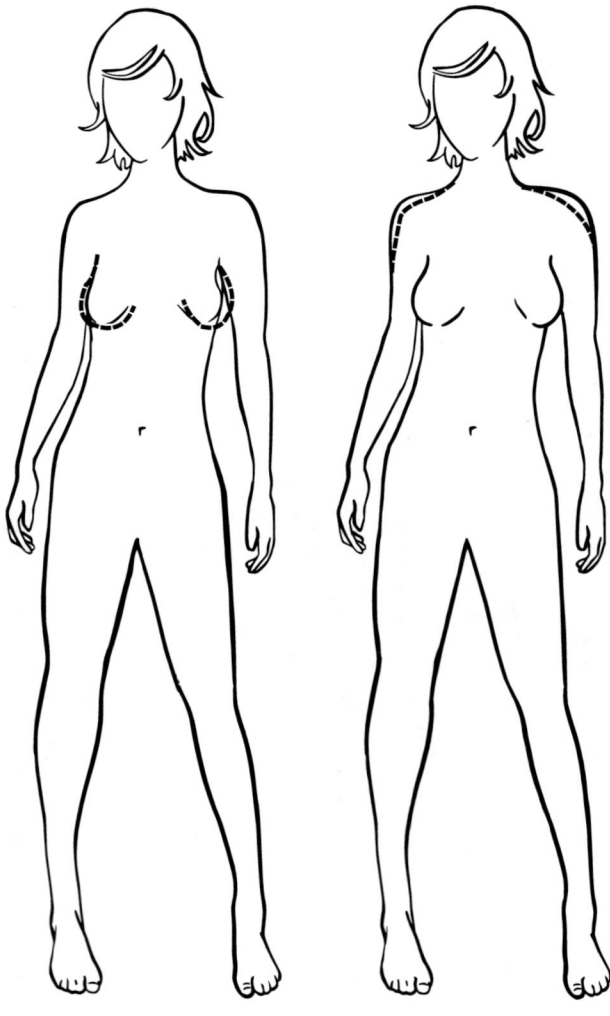

FIGURE 7-3

Small Breasts – Bust is narrower than hips and shoulders or smaller than you want them to be.

FIGURE 7-4

Wide Shoulders – Shoulders are wider than hips or wider than you want them to be.

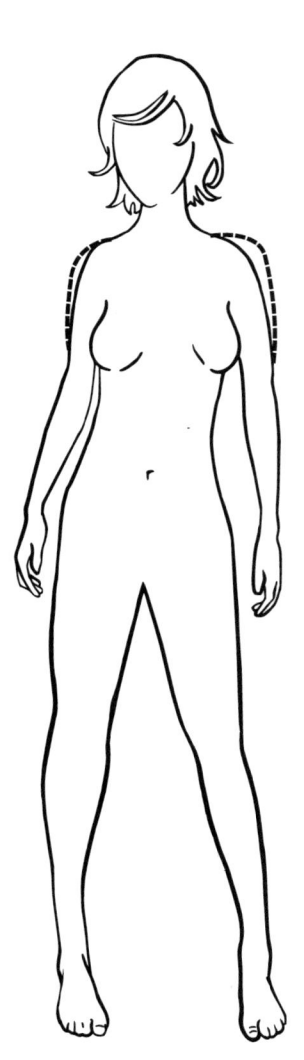

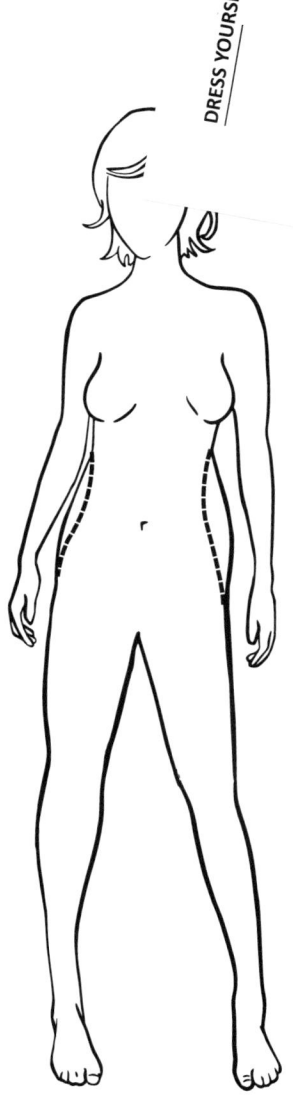

FIGURE 7-5

Narrow Shoulders –
Shoulders are more
narrow than hips or
more narrow than you
want them to be.

FIGURE 7-6

Tummy or Thick Waist –
Waist is wider than ¾ of the
width of hips and shoulders
or tummy protrudes from the
torso further than you'd like.

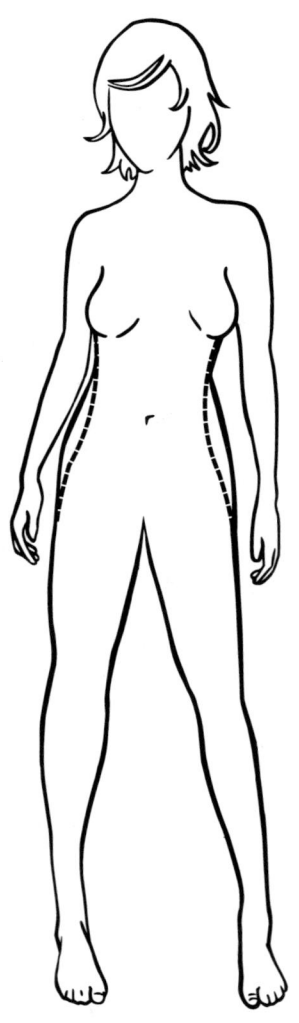

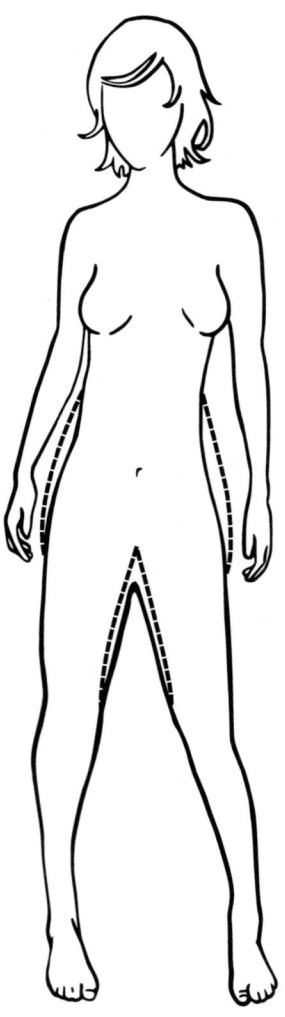

FIGURE 7-7	FIGURE 7-8

Short Waist or Short Torso –
Your bent elbow is below your waist and the distance from the top of your head to your hipbones is shorter than the distance from your hipbones to the floor.

Long Waist or Long Torso –
Your bent elbow is above your waist and the distance from the top of your head to your hipbones is longer than the distance from your hipbones to the floor.

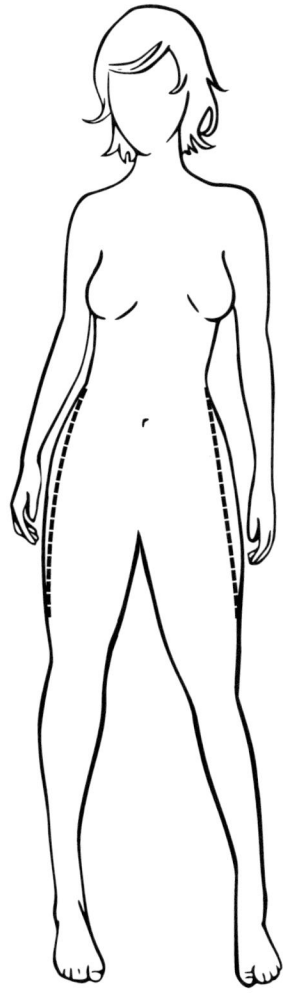 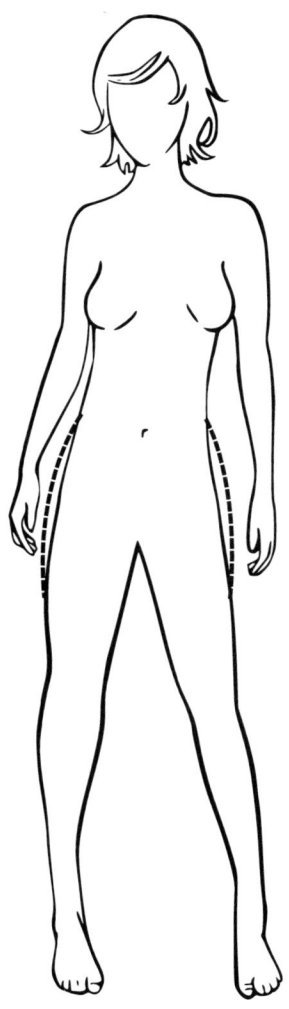

FIGURE 7-9

Wide Hips – Your bottom or hips are wider than your shoulders or wider than you'd like.

FIGURE 7-10

Narrow Hips – Your hips are more narrow than your shoulders or narrower than you'd like.

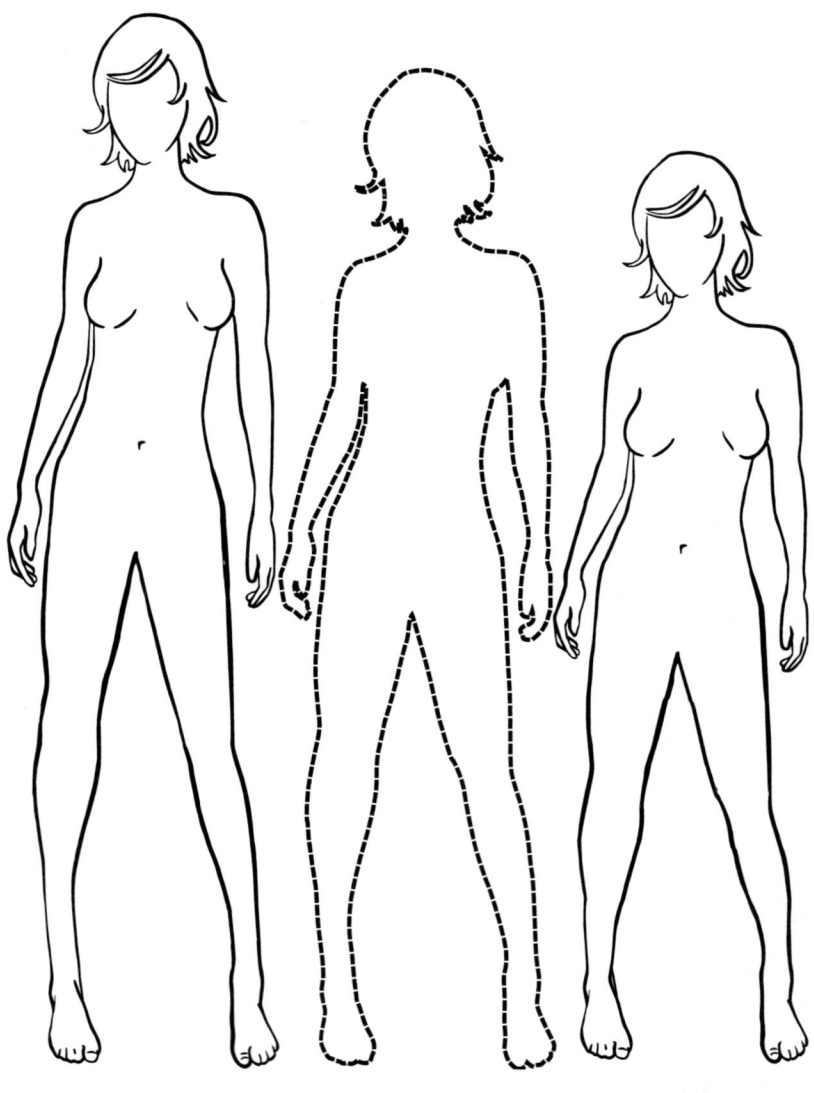

FIGURE 7-11	**IDEAL FIGURE**	**FIGURE 7-12**
Tall – You are taller than you want to be.		**Short** – You are shorter than you want to be.

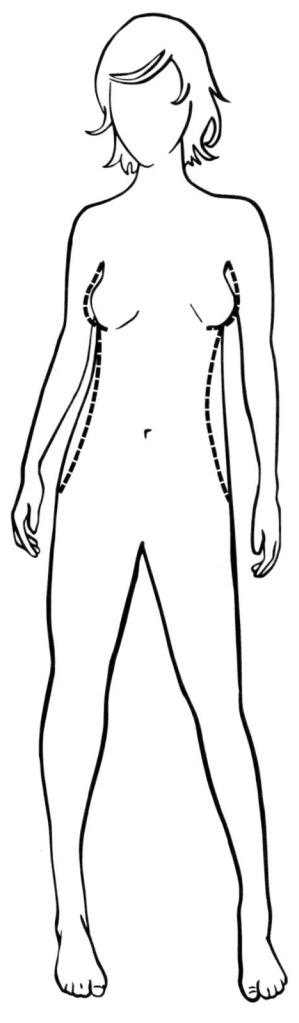

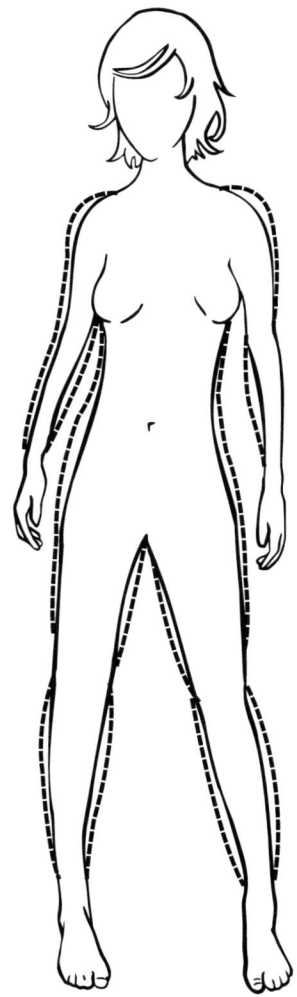

FIGURE 7-13

Straight Figure – The width of your bust, waist and hips are about the same or you are less curvy than you'd like to be.

FIGURE 7-14

Skinny – You are skinnier than you want to be.

CHAPTER 8
Stepping into the Hourglass

Transforming your body into an hourglass figure is all about the art of illusion. There are only three steps that stand between the body you have and the body you want: Maximize/minimize, Adjust and Distract.

Step 1 - Minimize or maximize that area of your body that is of concern. If the area is too big, then you'll make it look smaller. If the area is too small or narrow, then you'll make it look bigger.

Step 2 - Adjust the visual proportions of the body to balance the area of concern with the rest of you. If the area is too big, then you'll make other parts look bigger to balance it out. Yes, you read that right! You'll make other parts of your body look bigger. Don't worry! In the end, all of you will look smaller.

If your area of concern is too small, you'll make other parts of your body look smaller for balance.

In all cases, except the "skinny" body type, it's important to keep your waist visible so you don't add visual weight to your body. Keep tops narrow and close to the body in the waist area to accentuate the smallness of the waist. Also, button jackets just below the bust, at the most narrow part of the torso to make your waist appear smaller.

Step 3 – Divert Attention to your Good Parts. Distract attention away from the area of concern. When you attract attention to the body parts you like, the body parts you don't like become less noticeable. Use accessories or details, such as pleats, stitching, contrasting colors, piping, or beading, to pull attention away from the area of concern.

You can minimize the width of the area of concern by bringing attention to the centerline of the body. This works because you can't look two places at the same time. When you look at the centerline of the body, the outer edges of the body actually become blurry and obscure the real width of your body.

Each of the following chapters is organized by body type. Each contains suggestions for choosing and wearing clothing and accessories in a way that flatters your body. The strategies presented also apply to swimwear and lingerie. The advice works whether you are buying new pieces, sorting the items you already have or tailoring garments to make them work better for you.

Diagrams of specific tops, bottoms, dresses, jackets and accessories that flatter each body type are provided at the end of each chapter. As you sort your existing wardrobe, use these illustrations to guide you in what to keep in your closet or add to your shopping list.

If shopping is usually an unpleasant experience, bring along these diagrams to make the shopping experience easier and more efficient. Use the illustrations while you're shopping to identify styles that work for you and avoid the time and discomfort of trying on styles that don't work.

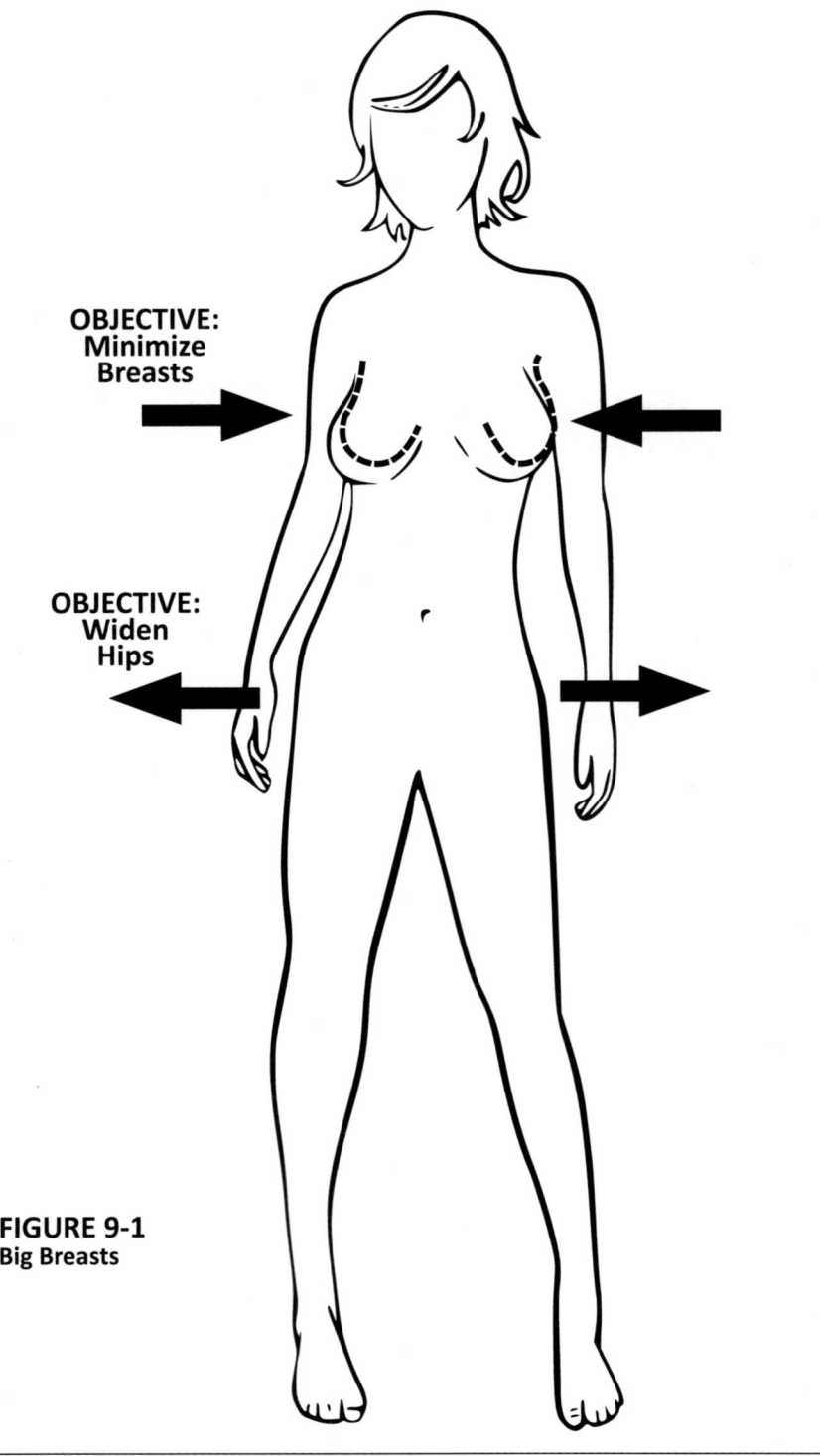

OBJECTIVE:
Minimize
Breasts

OBJECTIVE:
Widen
Hips

FIGURE 9-1
Big Breasts

CHAPTER 9
Big Breasts

Suzy has a full bust and used to wear oversized tops in an effort to minimize and camouflage her bustline. Her strategy backfired because it added bulk her waist and torso. The oversized tops made her look heavier than she really was. Here's what really works for women with big breasts.

Step 1 - Minimize The Bust

The first order of business is to get a bra that works. The right bra for you will minimize the size of the breasts, support them close to the body and lift them up and away from your waist. Tips for getting a great fitting bra are provided in Chapter 3.

Solid, dark colored tops minimize the bust. Choose tops that look smooth and float over the body without grabbing or gaping. Use wardrobe tape or have a tailor sew a snap or hook to keep blouses with buttons from gaping at the bustline. Avoid adding bulk around the shoulders or neckline by steering clear of ruching, ruffles, gathers or pleats around the neckline or bust. Also, skip puffy sleeves and shoulder pads.

Keep cleavage under wraps. Necklines should not reveal any cleavage, so stick to short V-necks, short scoop-necks, jewel necklines, boat-necks, asymmetrical one-shoulder tops and mandarin collars. Skip deep V-necks, deep scoop-necks and strapless necklines.

Step 2 - Adjust The Proportions

Narrow hips make the body look top-heavy, making the bust look even bigger. Adding some width to the hips balances the bust and makes breasts look smaller.

Widen the appearance of the hips by wearing bottoms with light colors, bold patterns or horizontal lines. Choose skirts and pants with side-seam pockets or ruching, gathers, pleats or ruffles near the hips. You also can wear a belt, sash or shawl in a contrasting color around the hips. Skinny cigarette pants, boot-cut pants, full skirts, bubble skirts, tiered skirts, pencil skirts, puffy skirts and skirts with a flounce or pleats at the hem also work well. Jackets and tops with a flare or peplum at hips also visually widen the hips.

Be sure to keep the waist in view so you don't add visual weight to your body. Keep tops narrow and close to the body in the waist area to accentuate the smallness of the waist. Button jackets just below the bustline, at the narrowest part of the torso to emphasize the waist.

Step 3 - Distract Attention From The Bustline

Wear accessories away from your bust to distract the eye away. Wear colorful or dangling earrings, rings, bracelets, belts or shoes. Choose a purse that hangs away from the bustline, such as a long shoulder bag, handbag or clutch bag. Avoid wearing a long shoulder bag across your chest.

TOPS:

Note: Tops should be darker than bottoms.

Jewel Neckline

Short Scoop Neckline

Short V-Neckline

Medium Scoop Neckline

Boat Neckline

Tunic

Fitted Waist

Mandarin Style

Short Stance 3-Button Fitted Jacket

One-shoulder

Jacket with Peplum

Button Jacket Just Below the Bustline

Top with Asymmetrical Shoulders

BOTTOMS:

Full Skirt

Layered Skirt

Cuff Short-Shorts with Big Details at Hips

Pencil Skirt with Plaid Stripes

Tiered Skirt

Pencil Skirt

Skirt with Big Details at Hip

Bubble Skirt

Cigarette/ Skinny Pants

Boot Cut Pants

Pants with Side Seam Pockets

DRESSES:

Wrap Dress

Dress with
Puffy Skirt

Dress with Fitted
Torso and Full Skirt

ACCESSORIES:

Dangling Earrings

Choker

Clutch Bag

Ring

Bracelet

Long Shoulder Bag

Handbag

SHOES:

Note: See chapter 5 for shoe styles and hairstyles.

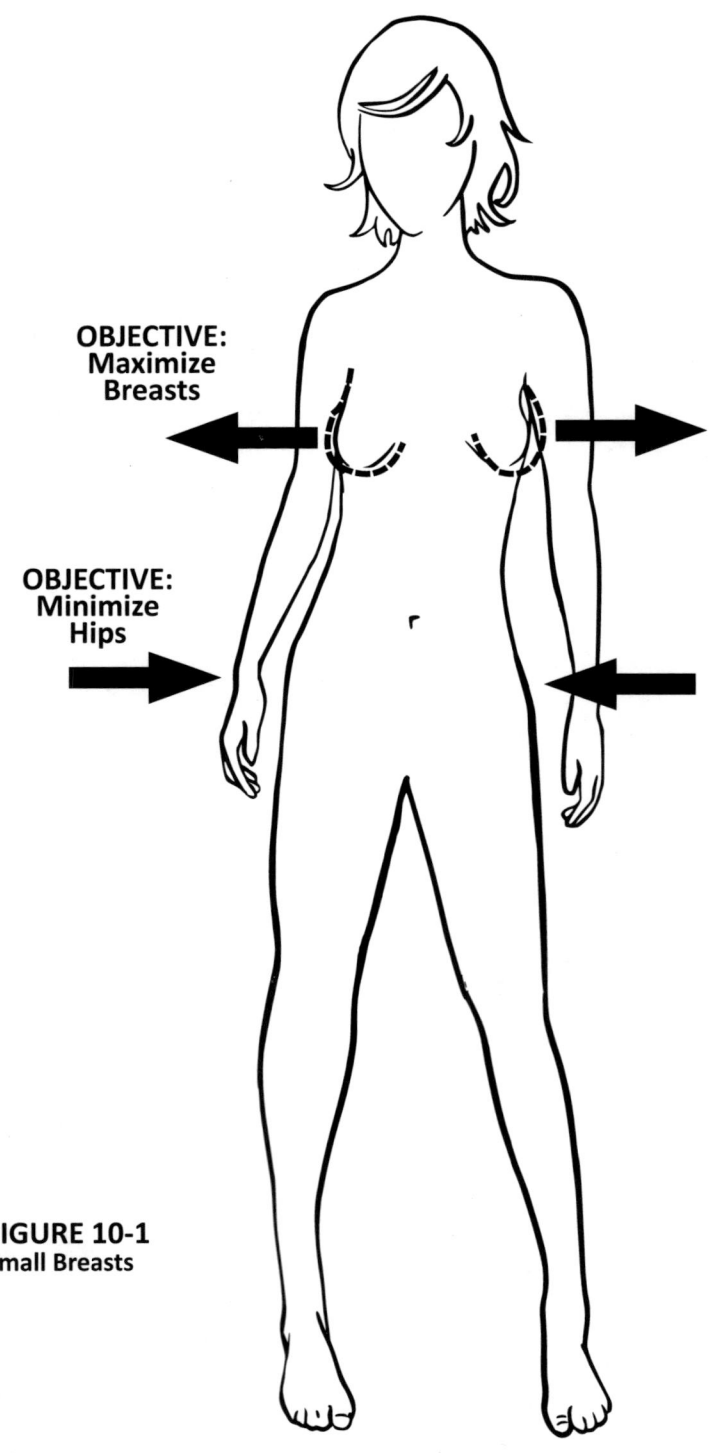

OBJECTIVE:
Maximize
Breasts

OBJECTIVE:
Minimize
Hips

FIGURE 10-1
Small Breasts

CHAPTER 10
Small Breasts

Rachel has small breasts. She wore tight tops in an effort to make the most of her tiny bustline. This approach didn't work because it actually emphasized the smallness or her breasts. Here's the right way to make small breasts look bigger.

Step 1 - Maximize The Bust
The right bra will make all the difference. Choose a "push-up" style that maximizes the size of the breasts, padded cups to make them look even bigger and lift them up and away from your waist. You also can place small half-moon shaped pads made from foam or silicon inside your bra for more volume. Fashion insiders call these pads "chicken cutlets."

Choose tops in light colors or bold patterns with cowl necks, breast pockets, ruching, smocking, ruffles, gathers, horizontal stripes, sequins, buttons, fringe or pleats along the neckline and bust area. These details will add physical and visual volume to the breasts.

Step 2 - Adjust The Proportions
Wide hips make the bust look smaller. Emphasizing your waist and making your hips look more narrow will make your bust area look bigger.

Emphasize the waist by wearing tops that lie close to the body without grabbing or gaping. This will accentuate the difference between the sizes of the bust and waist. Button your jackets just below the bustline, at the narrowest part of the torso to make the waist appear even smaller.

Narrow the appearance of the hips by wearing bottoms with darker colors or vertical lines. Choose A-line skirts and trouser-style pants that lie smoothly over the hips. Skip lighter colors on the bottom, side-seam pockets or ruching, gathers, pleats or ruffles near the hips. Steer clear of skinny cigarette pants, tapered "mom" pants, boot-cut pants, pencil skirts, bubble skirts and jackets with a flare or peplum at hips.

Step 3 - Distract Attention from the Bust Line

Wear accessories away from your bust, such as colorful or dangling ear-rings, rings, bracelets, belts or shoes. Choose a purse that hangs away from the bustline, such as a long shoulder bag, handbag or clutch bag.

Skip necklaces and avoid wearing a long shoulder bag across your chest.

TOPS:

Flutter Sleeves

Ruching at Bustline

Ruched Top

Peasant Top

Cowl Neckline

Ruffles at Bustline

Horizontal Stripes

Sequin Details at Neckline and Chest

Fringe Neckline

BOTTOMS:

Note: Bottoms should be darker than tops.

A-Line Skirt

Skirt with Box Pleats

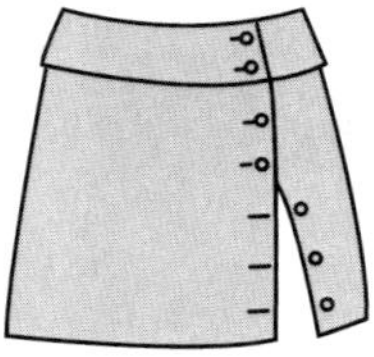

Skirt with Slit

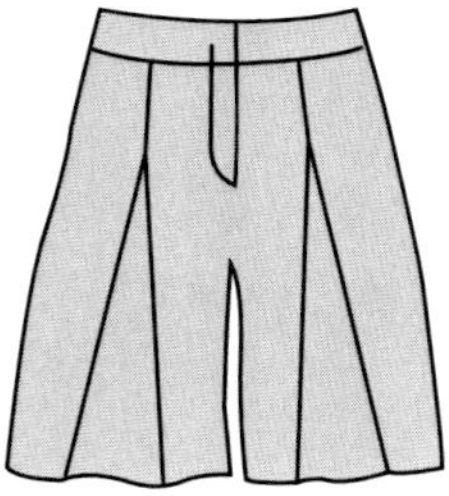

Walking Shorts

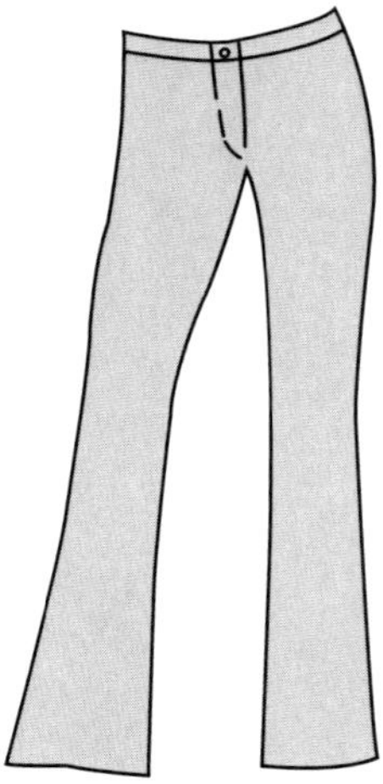

Boot Cut Pants

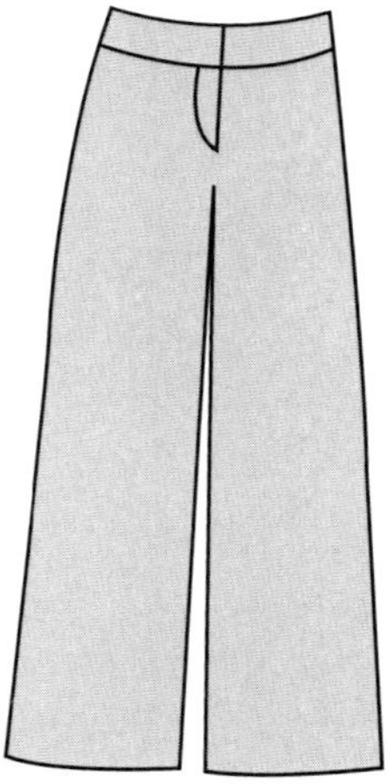

Flat Front Trousers

DRESSES:

Breast Pockets

Drop Waist Dress

ACCESSORIES:

Clutch Bag

Handbag

Long Shoulder Bag

Dangling Earrings

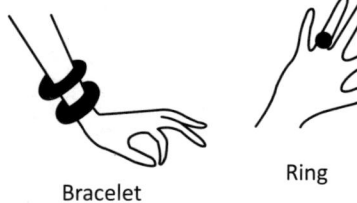

Bracelet

Ring

SHOES:

Note: See chapter 5 for shoe and hairstyles.

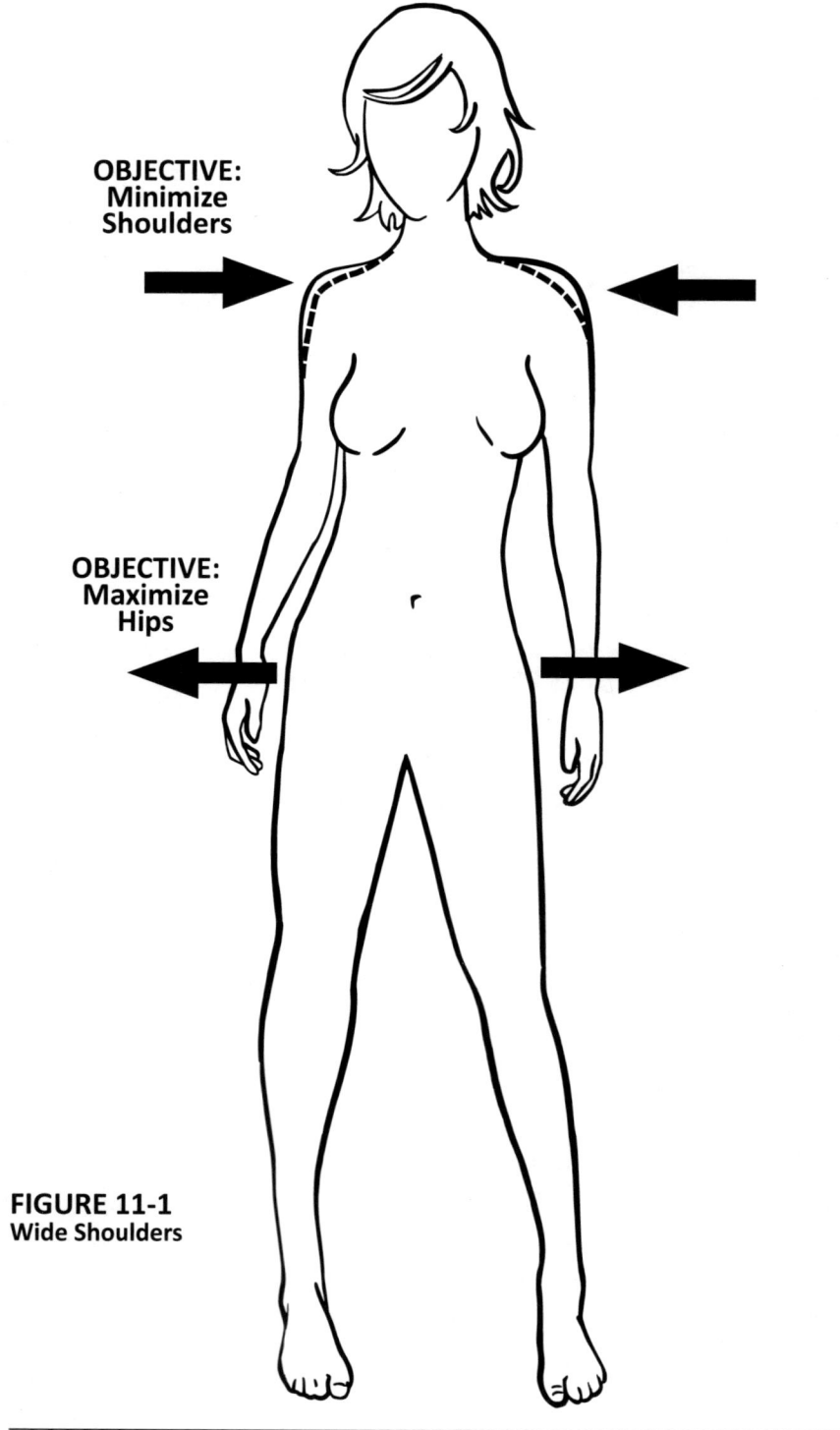

OBJECTIVE:
Minimize
Shoulders

OBJECTIVE:
Maximize
Hips

FIGURE 11-1
Wide Shoulders

CHAPTER 11

Wide Shoulders

Janet has wide shoulders. She used to wear jackets with shoulder pads and blouses with collars because that was her professional uniform. Unfortunately, the shoulder pads added bulk to her already prominent shoulders. The collar further emphasized her shoulders by "pointing" right at them. The overall effect made her look like Superman.

Here is what really works to make wide shoulders look more narrow.

Step 1 - Minimize the Shoulders to Make Them Appear More Narrow
Choose tops in medium to dark solid colors that emphasize the centerline of the body. Choose halter, one-shoulder, cold-shoulder, and collarless styles and styles with deep, V-necklines, scoop-necks and asymmetrical necklines. Details along these necklines will further emphasize the neckline rather than your shoulders.

Skip collars, puffy sleeves, shoulder pads, tube-tops or anything that creates a horizontal line on the torso, such as horizontal stripes, boat necks or square necklines.

Avoid accessories that emphasize the shoulders, such as dangling earrings, choker-style necklaces, shoulder bags and backpacks.

Step 2 - Adjust the Proportions
Narrow hips emphasize a wide upper body and make your shoulders appear wider. Add some width to your hips to balance the shoulders. Be sure to keep your waist visible so you don't add visual weight to your body.

Widen the appearance of your hips by wearing bottoms in fabrics with light colors, bold patterns or horizontal lines. Choose skirts and pants with side-seam pockets or ruching, gathers, pleats or ruffles near the hips. Wear a belt, sash or shawl in a contrasting color around the hips. Jackets and tops with flare or peplum at hips will visually widen the hips. Skinny cigarette pants, boot-cut pants, tiered skirts and skirts with a flounce or pleats at the hem also work well for you.

Step 3 - Distract Attention from the Shoulders

Move attention away from the shoulders and toward the face, cleavage and centerline of the body.

Wear accessories to distract the eye away from the shoulders, such as long necklaces with pendants, belts, bracelets, rings, shoes and long scarves. Choose a long shoulder bag worn across the body, a handbag or clutch bag.

Skip dangling earrings, choker style necklaces and backpack style bags.

TOPS:

Note: Tops should be darker than bottoms.

V-Neckline Without Collar or Lapels

One-Shoulder

Top with Asymmetrical Shoulders

One-Shoulder

Halter

Bare Shoulders

"Cold" Shoulder

V-Neckline

Scoop Neckline

Flared at Hips

Button Jacket Just Below the Bustline

Ruffle Pockets

Jacket/Top with Peplum

BOTTOMS:

Cuff Short-Shorts
Big Details at Hips

Layered Skirt

Bubble
Skirt

Skirt with Flounce/
Pleats at Hem

Skirt with
Big Details
at Hip

Full Skirt

Pants with Side
Seam Pockets

Cigarette/Skinny Pants
Flared at Hips

DRESSES:

Full Skirt

Mock Halter

Bare
Shoulder

Gathers
at Hip

ACCESSORIES:

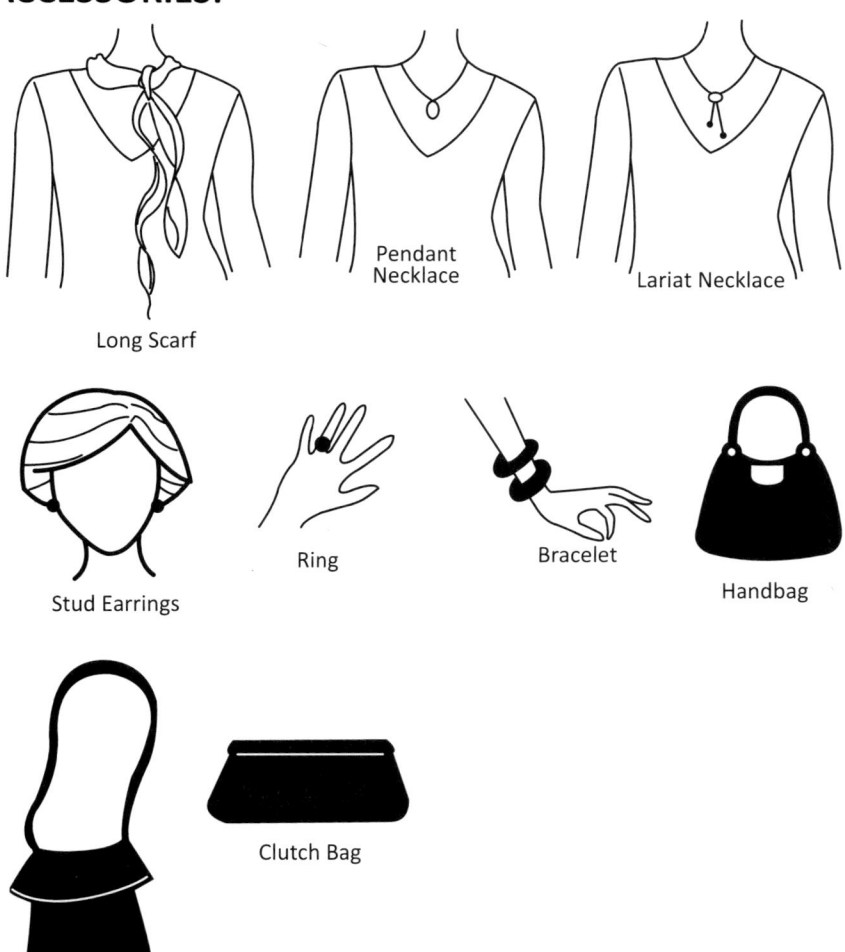

Long Scarf

Pendant
Necklace

Lariat Necklace

Stud Earrings

Ring

Bracelet

Handbag

Clutch Bag

Long Shoulder Bag

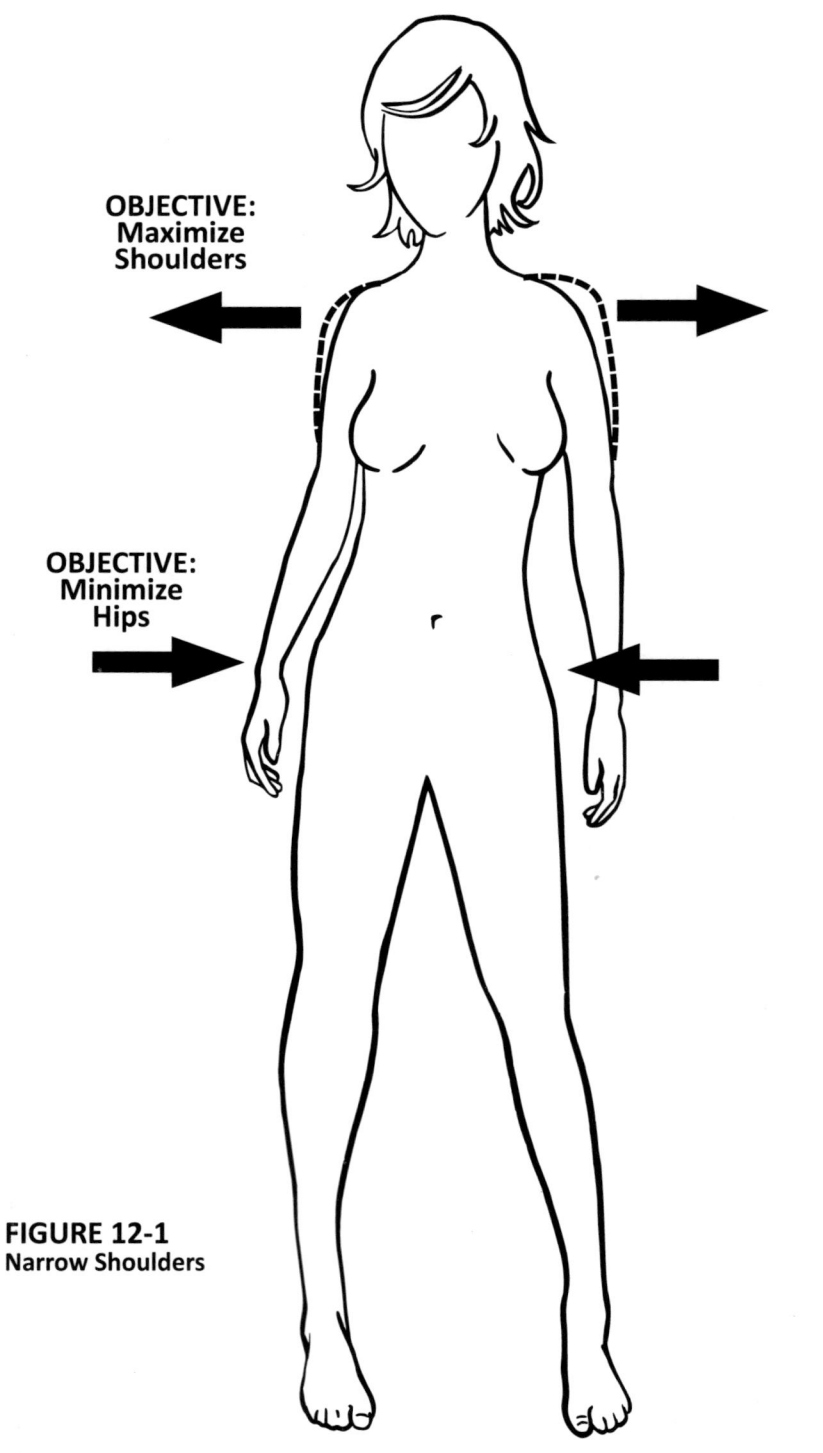

OBJECTIVE:
Maximize
Shoulders

OBJECTIVE:
Minimize
Hips

FIGURE 12-1
Narrow Shoulders

CHAPTER 12
Narrow Shoulders

Tiffany didn't realize that she had narrow shoulders and always got her tops and jackets in the same size as her pants. Her tops always were swimming on her and made her look heavier than she actually was. It's more flattering for Tiffany to buy tops and jackets that are the right size and fill out her upper body with shoulder pads or puffy sleeves. Here are the steps for balancing narrow shoulders.

Step 1 – Maximize and Broaden the Shoulders
Tops in light colors, horizontal stripes or bold patterns will make your shoulders appear wider. Choose off-the-shoulder, square or boat-neck necklines or shoulder embellishments, such as puffy sleeves, shoulder pads, epaulettes, batwing sleeves, flutter sleeves, shrugs, or short sleeves with tabs or cuffs. Shirts with collars and wrap dresses also work well.

Details around the necklines and sleeves will further widen the appearance of the shoulders. You also can wrap a pashmina or shawl around the shoulders. A backpack is the best bag for you because it makes the shoulders look wider.

Step 2 - Adjust the Proportions
Visually narrowing the waist and hips will make your shoulders appear wider. Be sure to keep the waist in view so you don't add visual weight to your body. Button your jackets and sweaters just below the bust to emphasize the smallest part of the torso.

Narrow the appearance of the hips by wearing bottoms with solid, darker colors or vertical lines. Choose A-line skirts, trouser-style or boot-cut pants that lay smoothly along the hips.

Skip side-seam pockets or ruching, gathers, pleats or ruffles near the hips. Steer clear of skinny cigarette pants, tapered "mom"pants, pencil skirts, bubble skirts, lighter colors on the bottom or jackets with a flare or peplum at hips.

Step 3 - Distract Attention From The Shoulders
Distract attention away from the shoulders and toward the face, cleavage and centerline of the body. Opt for low necklines and accessories, such as

stud earrings, long necklaces, pendant and lariat necklaces, long scarves, belts, bracelets, rings and colorful or embellished shoes.

Choose a backpack, handbag or clutch bag. Skip dangling earrings, choker-style necklaces and long shoulder bags.

TOPS:

Puffy Sleeves

Flutter Sleeve

Wide Shoulders

Boatneck/
Horizontal Neckline

Boat Neckline

Blouse with
Tab Cuffs

Top with Shrug

Sequin Details at
Neckline and Chest

Top with Epaulettes

Fringe Neckline

Top with Batwing Sleeve
(Sleeve begins at waist)

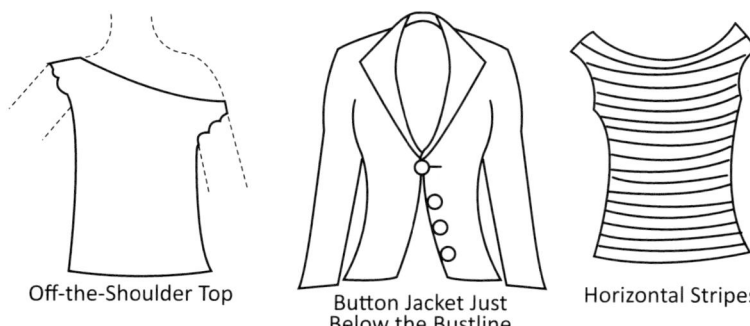

Off-the-Shoulder Top   Button Jacket Just   Horizontal Stripes
                         Below the Bustline

BOTTOMS:

Note: Bottoms should be darker than tops.

Skirt with Box Pleats    A-Line Skirt

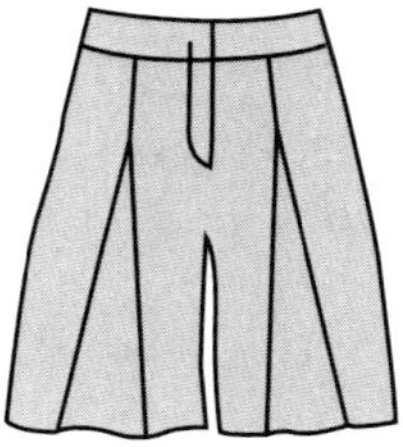

                                                     Walking Shorts

Skirt with Slit

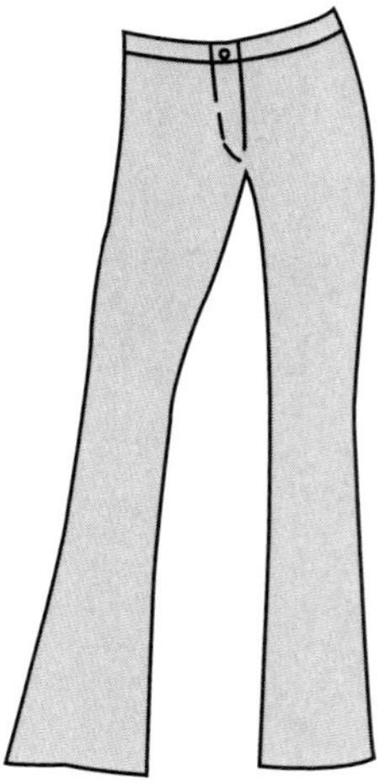

                          Boot Cut Pants

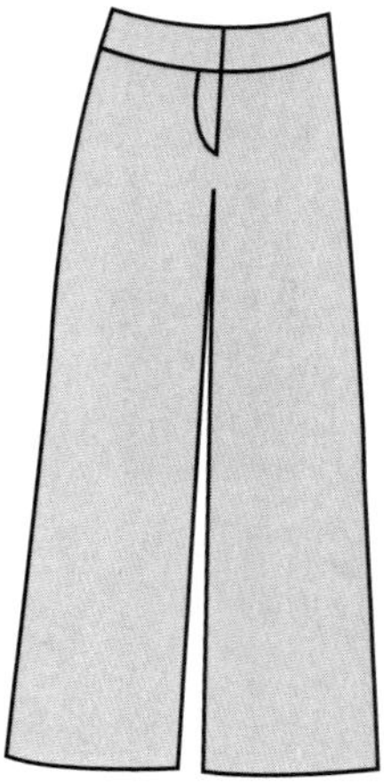

                                              Flat Front
                                              Trousers

DRESSES:

Shoulder Pads

Ruffle Sleeves

ACCESSORIES:

Note: See chapter 5 for shoe and hairstyles.

Pendant
Necklace

Long Scarf

Lariat Necklace

Handbag

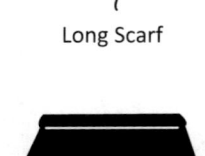

Clutch Bag

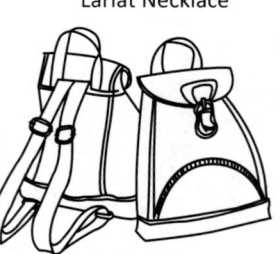

Backpack

Bracelet

Ring

Stud Earrings

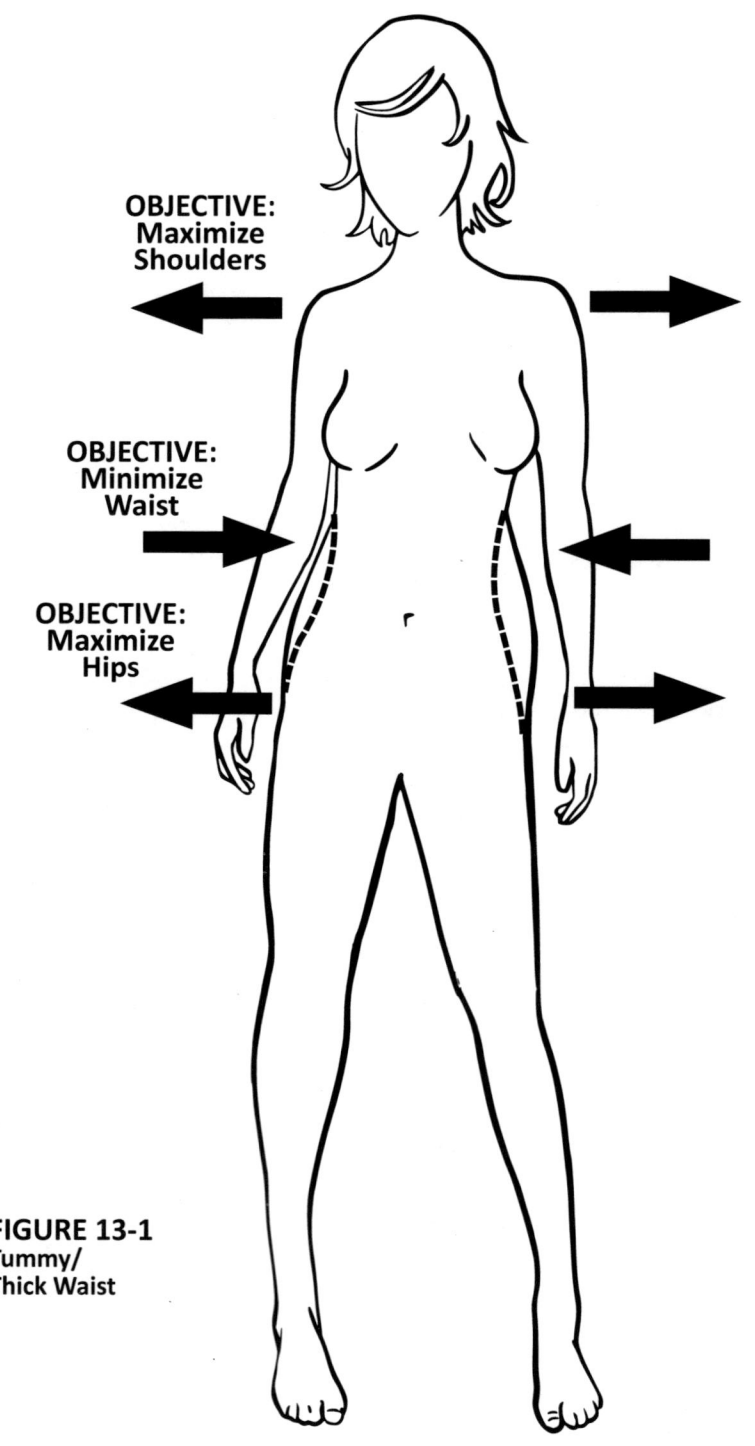

OBJECTIVE:
Maximize
Shoulders

OBJECTIVE:
Minimize
Waist

OBJECTIVE:
Maximize
Hips

FIGURE 13-1
Tummy/
Thick Waist

CHAPTER 13

Tummy or Thick Waist

Tina used to wear loose shirts and pleated pants to camouflage her tummy. Instead of hiding her belly, these clothes actually made her tummy look bigger by adding extra fabric and bulk to the tummy and waist area. Here is the right way to make the tummy and waist look smaller.

Step 1 - Minimize the Waist and Tummy

A great-fitting bra is critical to creating the illusion of a small waist. The breasts should be supported so they are lifted up and away from the waist. When the breasts sag, they make your waist look wider than it really is. Tips for getting a great fitting bra are provided in Chapter 3.

Choose slim-fitting tops that skim the body and are snug around the ribcage, just below the bust. This is the smallest part of every woman's body and emphasis on this area will make your waist look smaller. Tops should be snug enough to skim along the body, but loose enough so they don't grab any rolls around the waist and tummy, gape at buttons or pull at seams.

Choose tops in darker colors. Opt for deep V-necks and scoop-necks, surplice (cross-over), tailored tunics, empire waists, trumpet sleeves and ombre fabric with the lighter color at bust and the darker color at the waist. Tops with gathers and ruching around the waist and tummy also work well to camouflage the area by making any tummy rolls look like they are part of the clothing.

Choose bottoms that smooth the tummy and don't add any bulk to the area. Flat-front pants and skirts with wide, smooth waistbands work well. Side zippers are best, but zippers in the front can work, too, if they lie very flat.

Avoid light-colored tops, tops that are longer than three inches below your hipbones and voluminous tops like peasant tops, batwing sleeves and trapeze styles, tops with waist bands or belts, horizontal stripes, bow-tie blouses and boxy jackets or sweaters. Skip pants and skirts with gathers, pleats, elastic or drawstrings at the waist. These styles all add volume to the torso and make you look heavier.

Step 2 - Adjust The Proportions

Visually narrow your waist by widening the appearance of your shoulders and hips.

Broaden the appearance of the upper body and shoulders by choosing off-the-shoulder, square or boat-neck necklines or add puffy sleeves, shoulder pads, epaulettes or short sleeves with tabs or cuffs.

Details along necklines and sleeves or a shawl wrapped around the shoulders will further widen the appearance of the shoulders. The best bag for you is a backpack because it emphasizes the tips of the shoulders.

Widen the appearance of the hips by wearing bottoms with light colors, bold patterns or horizontal lines. Choose skirts and pants with gathers, pleats or ruffles near the hips. A-line skirts and skirts with a flounce or ruffle at the hem also work well. Jackets and tops with a flare or peplum at hips also visually widen the hip area.

Step 3 - Distract Attention from the Waist

Move the attention away from the waist and toward the face, shoulders, cleavage and centerline of the body.

Low necklines, accessories that draw attention away from the waist and items that emphasize a vertical line all work well. Choose long, dangling earrings, necklaces with pendants and lariat-styles, long vertical scarves, bracelets, rings, embellished or colorful shoes and clutch bags or handbags.

Skip belts at the waist and shoulder bags that hang near the waist because they bring attention to the waist and tummy.

TOPS:

Note: Tops should be darker than bottoms.

Fitted at
Rib Cage

Untucked
Blouses

Jackets/Tops
with Peplum

Puffy Sleeves

Epaulettes
at Shoulders

Blouse with
Tab Cuffs

Empire
Waist

Empire Waist

Top with
Trumpet Sleeve

Boat Neckline

Scoop Neckline

V-Neckline

Asymmetrical Neckline

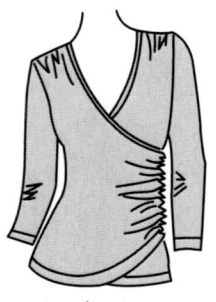

Surplice Top

Tunic

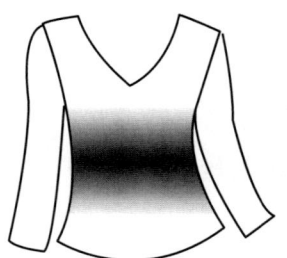

Ombre with darkest
tones at waist

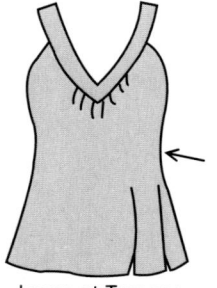

← Fitted
at Rib
Cage

Loose at Tummy

BOTTOMS:

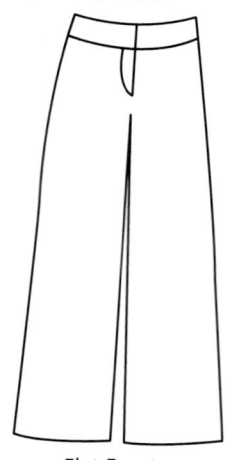

Flat Front
Trousers

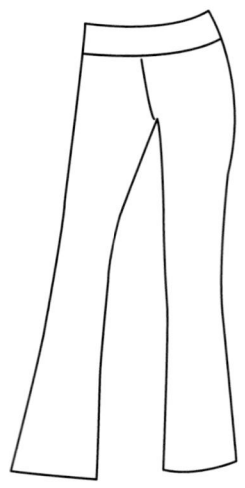

Side Zip Pants

Skirt with Big
Details at Hip

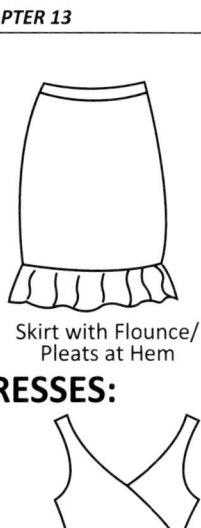

Skirt with Flounce/
Pleats at Hem

A-Line Skirt

Skirt with Box Pleats

DRESSES:

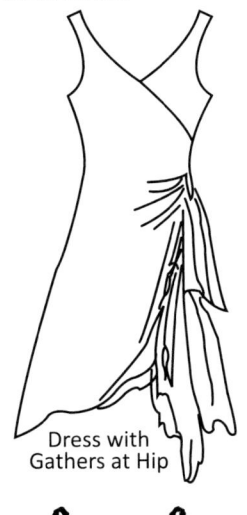

Dress with
Gathers at Hip

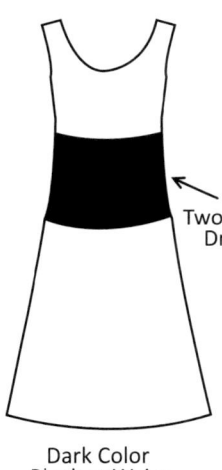

Two-Tone
Dress

Dark Color
Block at Waist

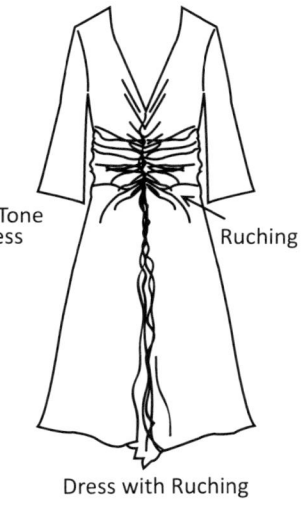

Ruching

Dress with Ruching

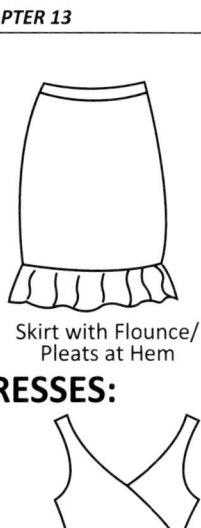

Empire
Waist

Dress with Empire Waist

ACCESSORIES:

Note: See chapter 5 for shoe styles and hairstyles.

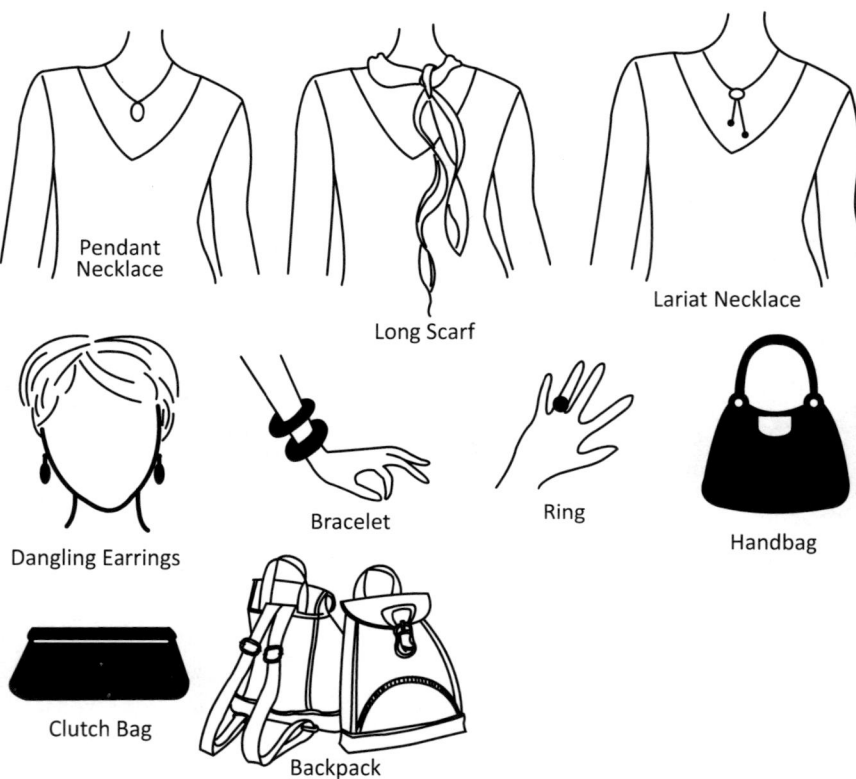

Pendant Necklace

Long Scarf

Lariat Necklace

Dangling Earrings

Bracelet

Ring

Handbag

Clutch Bag

Backpack

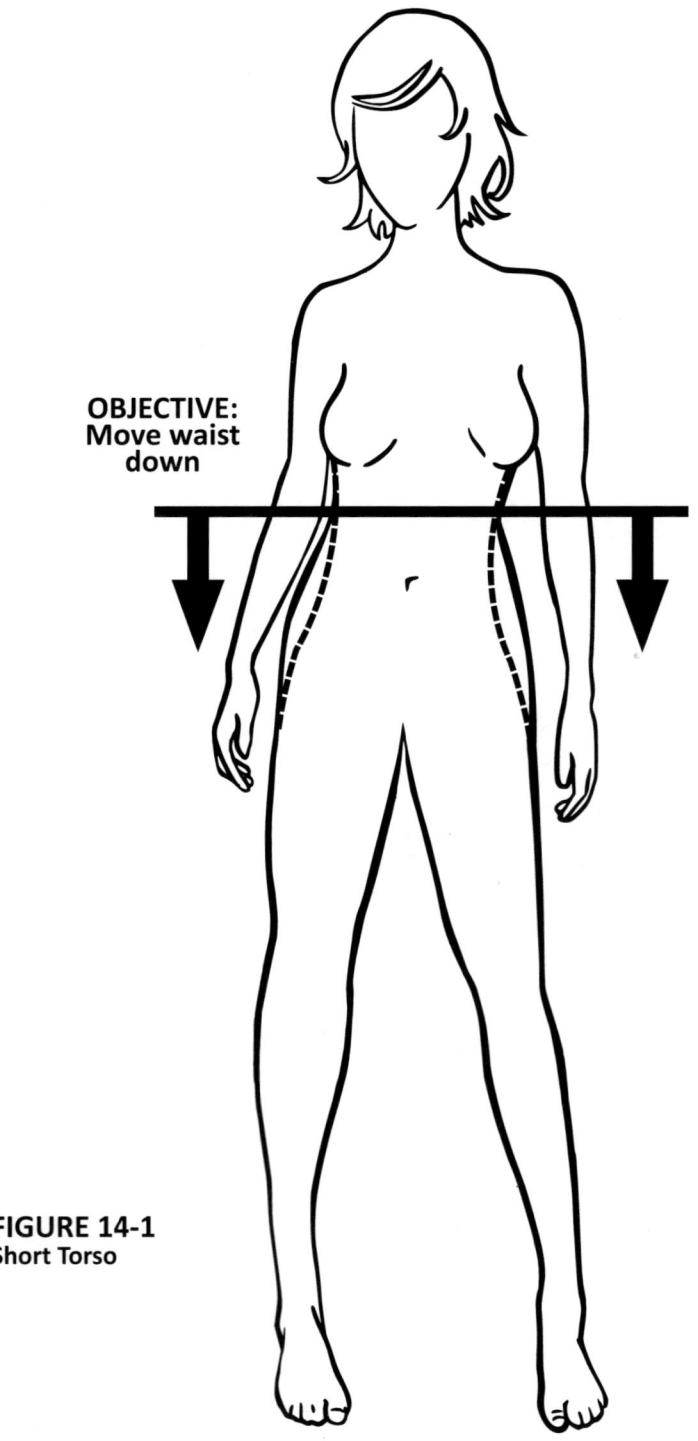

OBJECTIVE:
Move waist
down

FIGURE 14-1
Short Torso

CHAPTER 14
Short Torso or Short Waist

Theresa has a short torso. She tucks all her tops and sweaters into the waistbands of pants and skirts because she was taught that was the neat and proper way to dress. This approach doesn't work for short-waisted women because it makes your bustline and waistline look like they are right on top of each other and makes your torso look even shorter.

Here are the three steps to making your torso look longer.

Step 1 – Maximize the Length of Your Torso
A great fitting bra is critical for you. The breasts should be lifted up and away from the waist. When the breasts sag, they make your breasts and waist look like they are in the same place. Lifting the breasts defines your bustline and separates it from your waistline, making the torso look longer. Tips for getting a great fitting bra are provided in Chapter 3.

Choose tops in a contrasting color or print from the bottoms. Opt for tops that are narrow and close to the body in the waist area to make a distinction between the bust, waist and hip areas. Keep tops untucked with hemlines 2 to 3 inches below your the hipbones. This makes the torso look longer by extending it to the hips, instead of stopping at the waist.

Choose tops that emphasize vertical lines – look for V-necks, scoop necks, vertical or diagonal stripes and prints, princess seams, button-down shirts with contrasting stitching along the button placket and vertical appliqués, pleats, ruffles or lace. Wrap, crossover, surplice, empire waist and tailored tunics style tops all work great.

Try petite-sized tops because petite proportions may fit your torso length better than missy sizes. Also, have the hems of tops shortened and the location of the waist adjusted by a tailor so they fall at the right place for you.

Step 2 - Adjust the Proportions

Visually lengthen your torso by lowering the waistline of pants, skirts and dresses. Wear belts at the hips. Choose bottoms with a low to mid-rise waist and dresses and skirts with a drop-waist. Empire waist tops and dresses also can work well because they completely obscure the actual waistline. The hems of skirts and dresses should be at the knee or just below.

Never tuck in your shirt, ever. Skip high-waisted skirts and pants, visible waist-bands and anything belted at the waist.

Step 3 - Distract Attention from the Waist

Move attention away from the waist and toward the face, shoulders, cleavage or feet. Details around the necklines, sleeves or hems will distract attention away from the waistline.

Choose low necklines, long dangling earrings, pendant and lariat necklaces, long vertical scarves, hip belts, bracelets, rings, clutch bags and handbags.

Make sure the tails of long scarves hang unevenly and skip all belts around the waist.

TOPS:

Scoop Neckline

V-Neckline

Surplice Top

Tunic

Untucked
Blouses
Vertical Pin Stripes

Vertical Details

Jacket Fitted
at Rib Cage

Princess Seams

Empire
Waist

Top with
Empire Waist

Untucked Top

Fringe
Neckline

Sequin Details
at Neckline

BOTTOMS:

A-Line Skirt

Skirt with
Box Pleats

Walking Shorts

Slit Skirt

Boot Cut Low-Rise
Pants

Flat Front Low-Rise
Trousers

DRESSES:

Empire
Waist

Dress with
Empire Waist

Drop Waist Dress

ACCESSORIES:

Note: See chapter 5 for shoe styles and hairstyles.

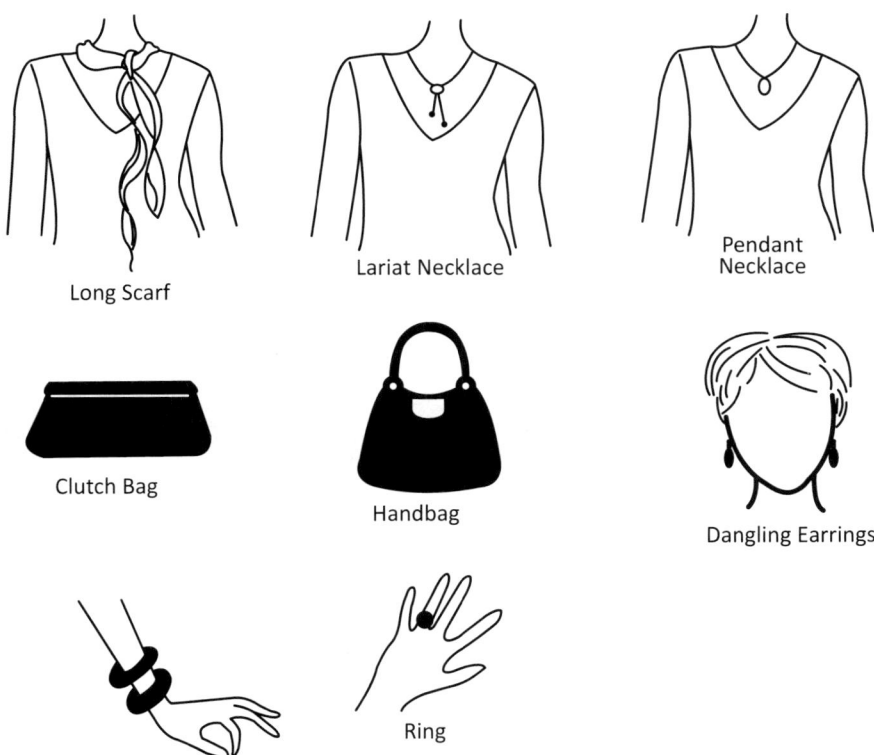

Long Scarf

Lariat Necklace

Pendant
Necklace

Clutch Bag

Handbag

Dangling Earrings

Bracelet

Ring

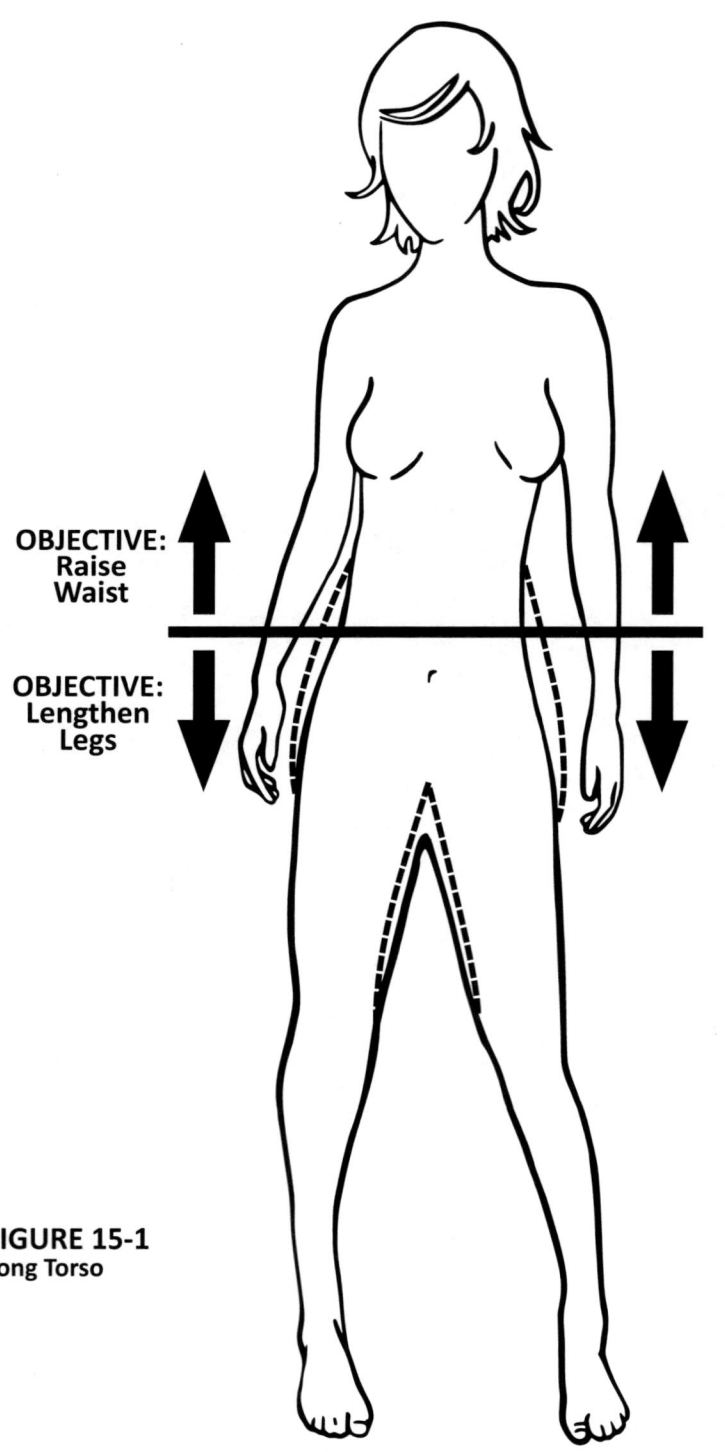

OBJECTIVE:
Raise
Waist

OBJECTIVE:
Lengthen
Legs

FIGURE 15-1
Long Torso

CHAPTER 15

Long Torso or Long Waist

Jeanette has a long torso. She wears her tops untucked because it makes her feel like her torso is covered. This strategy doesn't work because it makes her legs look shorter and her torso look even longer.

Here are the steps to make your torso and waist look shorter and your legs look longer.

Step 1 – Minimize (Shorten) the Torso

Tuck your tops into your pants and skirts, always. Choose high-waisted pants, skirts and dresses. These styles shorten your torso by raising the waistline and make the torso look like it stops at the bottom of your ribcage instead of extending all the way to your navel.

De-emphasize the location of the natural waistline by choosing tops in a color, tone or print that are similar to the bottoms. Choose tops that emphasize horizontal lines and blur the distinction between the neckline, bustline, waistline and hips. Tops with an empire waist work especially well because they visually lift the waistline. Wide belts and corset belts also can be worn just under the ribcage or at the natural waist.

Step 2 - Adjust the Proportions

Lengthen the appearance of your legs to balance the proportions of your torso.

Wearing high-heel or platform shoes is an easy way to lengthen your legs. The hems of skirts and dresses should be at or just above the knee, so plenty of leg is exposed. Pants should be as long as possible, with hems no more than ¾-inch above the floor at the heel. No matter what shoes you wear, make sure pant hems are long enough to accommodate the heel height.

Use these color tips to lengthen your legs:
- When wearing pants, wear socks or panty hose and shoes in the same color as your pants.
- When wearing skirts or shorts with tights, wear tights and shoes in the same color or tone as the skirt/shorts.
- When wearing skirts or shorts with sheer hosiery, wear hosiery and shoes in the same color as your skin.

- When wearing skirts or shorts with bare legs, wear shoes in the same color tone as your skin.

Skip low-rise skirts and pants, drop-waisted dresses and skirts, cropped pants, tunics and long jackets. Never untuck your shirt, ever. These styles make your legs look shorter and make your torso look even longer.

Avoid creating any vertical lines above the waist because they will make your torso longer. Skip pin striped tops, dangling earrings, pendant and lariat style necklaces, long scarves and shoulder bags.

Step 3 - Distract Attention from the Waist

Move the attention away from your waist and to your face, shoulders, cleavage or feet.

Details around the necklines and sleeves or hems of pants and skirts will distract attention away from the waistline.

Choose high necklines, big stud or hoop earrings, necklaces without pendants, short scarves tied at the neck, bracelets, rings, embellished shoes, clutch bags and handbags. Thick belts can be worn above the natural waist.

TOPS:

Horizontal Stripes

Jewel Neckline

Sweaters that Emphasize Waist/Rib Cage

Short Tops & Sweaters

Empire Waist Top

Empire Waist

Short Scoop Neckline

Short V-Neckline

Turtle Neck

Tuck in Tops

Tuck in Tops

BOTTOMS:

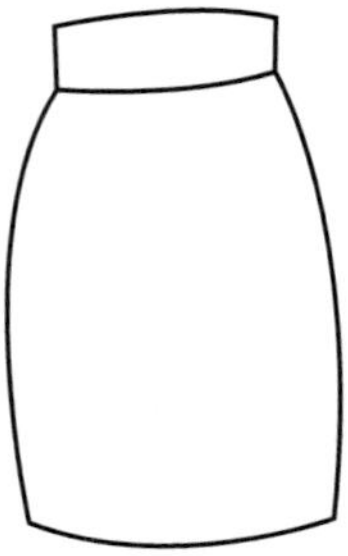

High-Waisted
Skirt

Walking Shorts

High-Waist
Boot Cut Pants

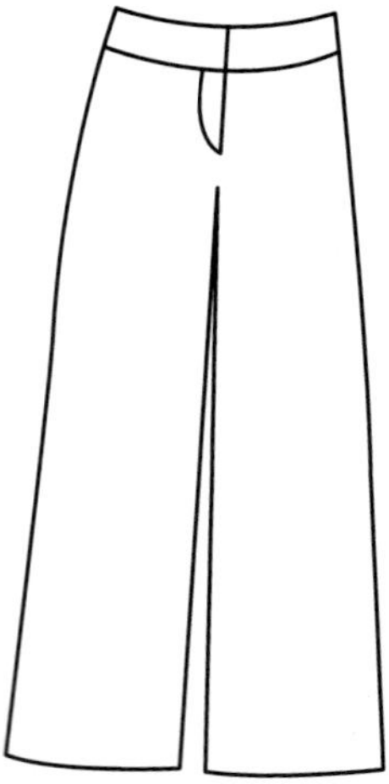

High-Waist
Flat Front
Trousers

DRESSES:

Dress with
Full Skirt

Color Block Dress

Dark Color
Block at
Waist

Empire Waist Dress

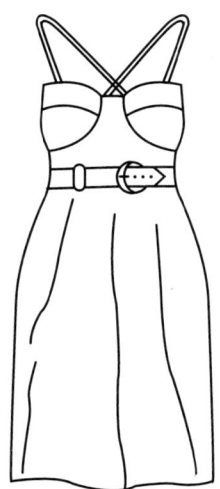

High-Waist Dress

Dress with
No Emphasis
on Waist

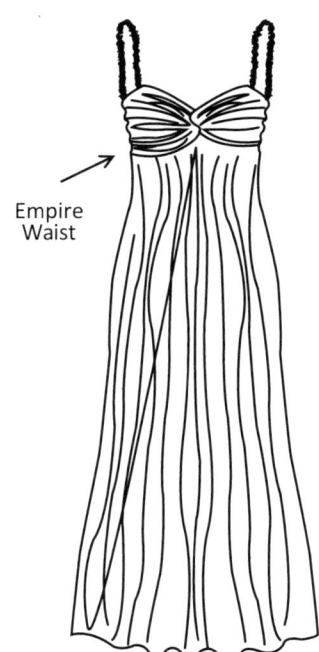

Empire
Waist

Empire Waist Dress

ACCESSORIES:

Handbag

Stud Earrings

Hoop Earrings

Clutch Bag

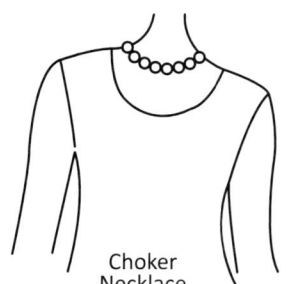

Choker
Necklace

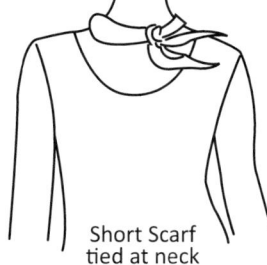

Short Scarf
tied at neck

HAIRSTYLES:
Note: See chapter 5 for hairstyles.

SHOES:

Kitten Heel Mule

Wedge Heel
Flip Flop

Closed-Toe
Mule

Knee Boot

Open-Toe Pump

Pump

Slingback
Sandal

Open-Toe Wedge Heel

Closed-Toe
Sling Back

High Heel Mule

Platform Pump

Open-Toe Platform
Sling Back

Wedge Heel Mule

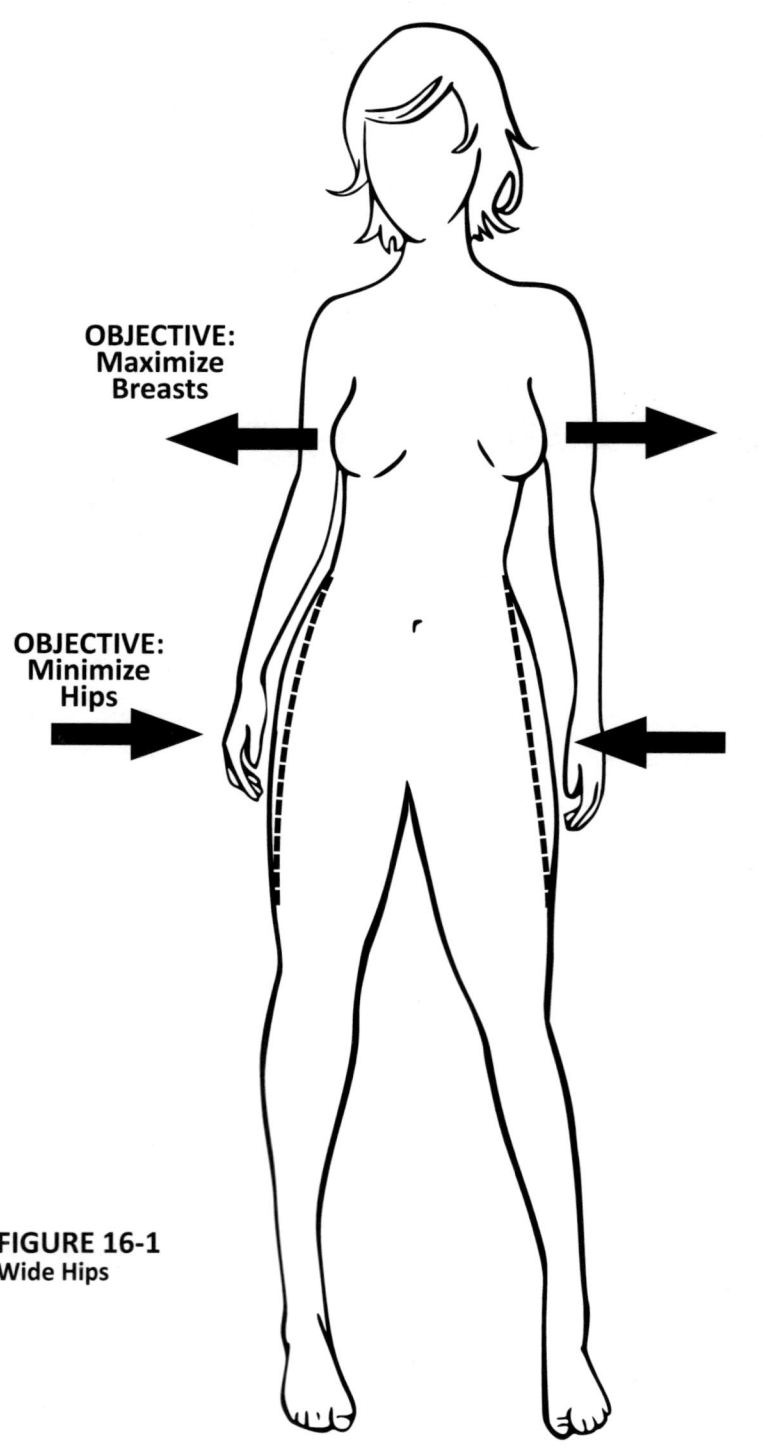

OBJECTIVE:
Maximize
Breasts

OBJECTIVE:
Minimize
Hips

FIGURE 16-1
Wide Hips

CHAPTER 16

Wide Hips or Big Bottom

Jill has big hips. She wears long jackets in an effort to cover and hide her wide hips and derriere. Instead of camouflaging, the jacket acts like a big billboard bringing more attention to the area. Long jackets and over-sized shirts add more volume to the body and make you look heavier than you are. Here's how to really slim your hips.

Step 1 - Minimize the Hips
Narrow the appearance of the hips by wearing bottoms in darker colors or with vertical lines. Choose bottoms that lay smoothly along the hips, such as A-line skirts, trouser-style pants and bottoms with zippers on the side.

Skip lighter colors on the bottom and bottoms with side-seam pockets or ruching, gathers, pleats or ruffles near the hips. Steer clear of skinny ciga-rette pants, tapered pants, pencil skirts, bubble skirts and jackets with a flare or peplum at hips. Also avoid pants with noticeable back pockets, i.e. with contrasting stitching, horizontal lines, embellishments or pocket flaps.

Step 2 - Adjust the Proportions
Widening the appearance of your shoulders will visually narrow your hips.

Widen the shoulders by choosing tops in light colors, bold patterns or horizontal stripes. Opt for tops with off-the-shoulder, square or boat-neck necklines, puffy sleeves, shoulder pads, epaulettes, batwing sleeves and short sleeves with tabs/cuffs or shrugs.

A bright colored pashmina or shawl wrapped around your shoulders will further widen the appearance of the shoulders. Be sure to keep the waist in view so you don't add visual weight to your body.

Step 3 - Distract Attention from the Hips

Distract attention away from your hips and toward your face, shoulders, cleavage, waist and centerline of the body.

Details around the necklines or sleeves will make hips less noticeable. Opt for low necklines, long dangling earrings, long pendant and lariat-style necklaces, belts at the waist, bracelets, rings, shoes, long scarves, clutch bags and handbags. A backpack is the best bag for you because it emphasizes the tips of the shoulders.

Skip hip belts and long shoulder bags because they bring too much attention to the area.

TOPS:

Asymmetrical
Neckline

Boat Neckline

Blouse with
Tab Cuffs

Top with Epaulettes

Puffy Sleeves

Batwing Sleeve
(Sleeve begins at waist)

Flutter Sleeve

Shrug

Boat/Horizontal
Neckline

Top with
Wide Shoulders

Horizontal Stripes

BOTTOMS:

Note: Bottoms should be darker than tops.

A-Line Skirt

Skirt with
Box Pleats

Slit Skirt

Walking Shorts

Pin Stripe Pants

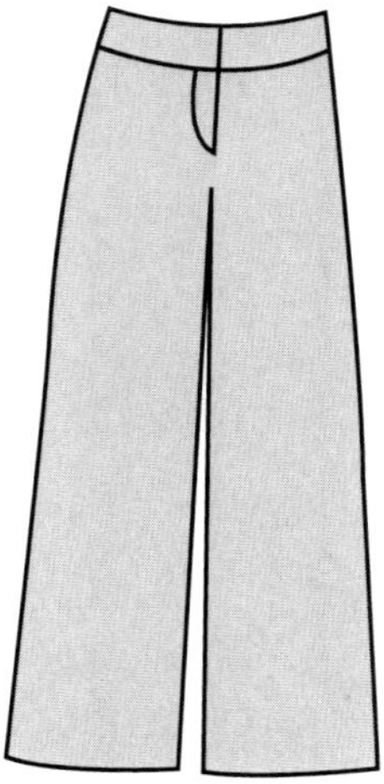

Flat Front Trousers

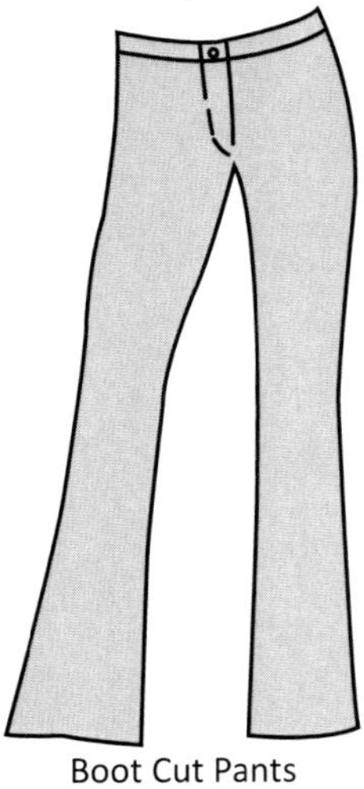

Boot Cut Pants

DRESSES:

A-line Dress

Dress with
Shoulder Pads

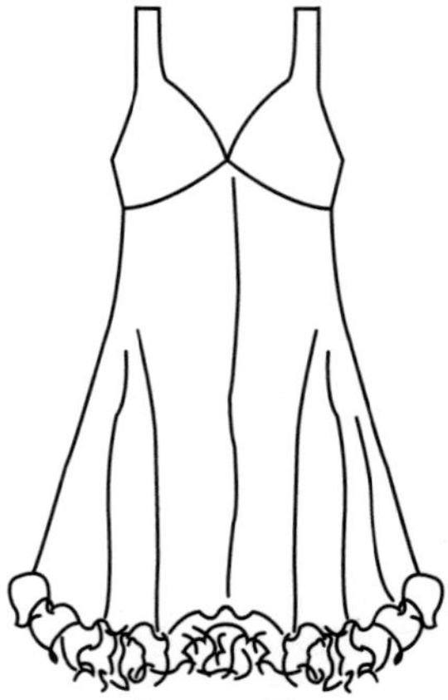

Dress with
No Emphasis
on Hips

Dress with
Ruffle Sleeves

Strapless Dress
with Fitted Waist

ACCESSORIES:

Note: See chapter 5 for shoe styles and hairstyles.

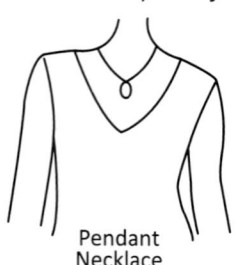

Pendant
Necklace

Long Scarf

Lariat Necklace

Backpack

Handbag

Clutch Bag

Dangling Earrings

Bracelet

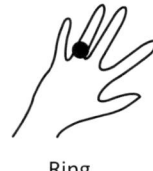

Ring

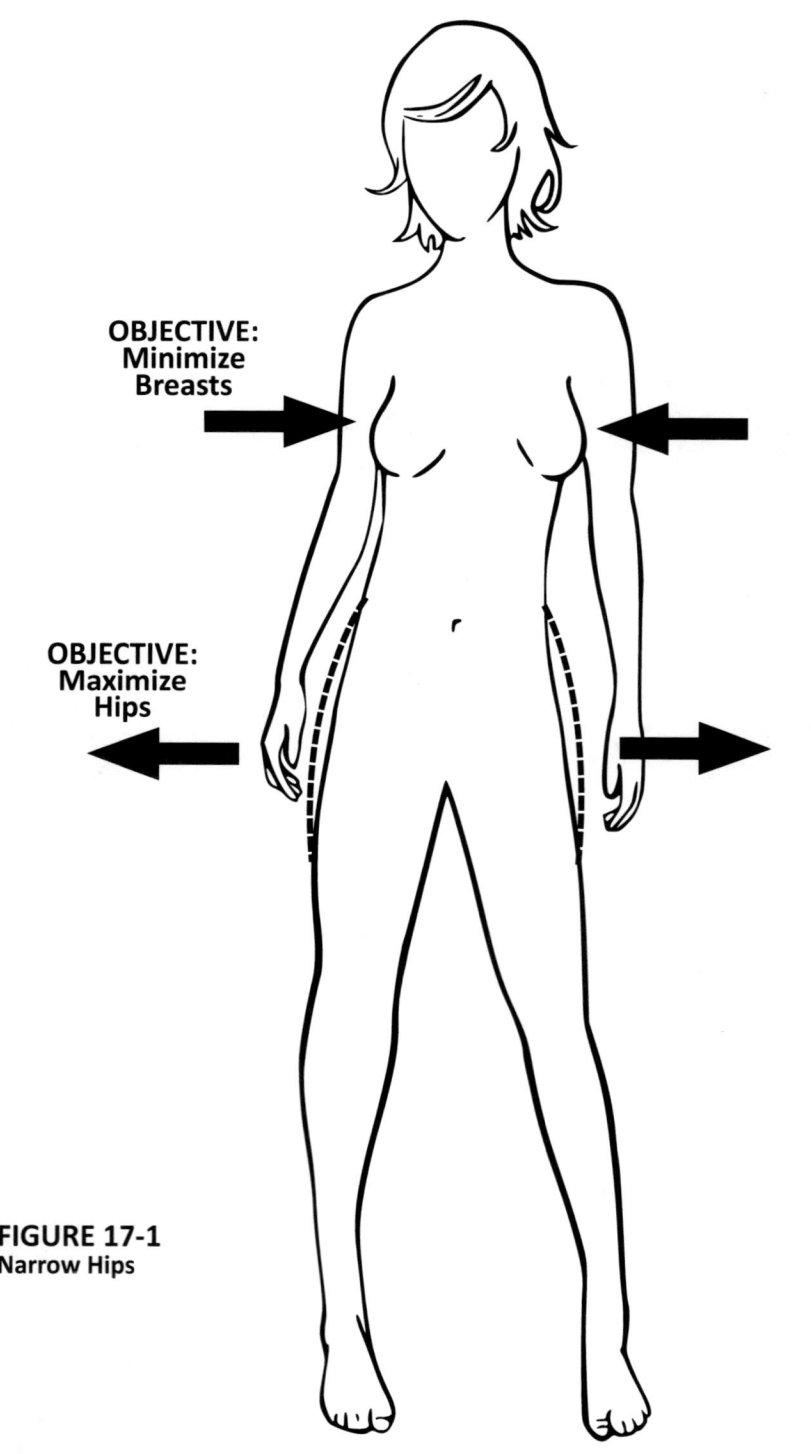

OBJECTIVE:
Minimize
Breasts

OBJECTIVE:
Maximize
Hips

FIGURE 17-1
Narrow Hips

CHAPTER 17

Narrow Hips

Norma has narrow hips. She wears slim fitting pants and skirts because she feels like they fit her figure well. Snug fitting bottoms emphasize the narrowness of her hips and erase any hint of curves. Here are the steps for making narrow hips appear more curvy.

Step 1 – Maximize and Widen the Hips

Widen the appearance of the hips by wearing bottoms with light colors, bold patterns or horizontal lines.

Choose skirts and pants with side-seam pockets, small back pockets, back pockets with flaps or ruching, gathers, pleats or ruffles near the hips. Choose skinny cigarette pants, bubble skirts, full skirts, tiered skirts and skirts and dresses with a flounce or ruffle at the hem. Jackets and tops with a flare or peplum at the hips also will visually widen the hips.

Wearing a belt, sash or shawl in a contrasting color around the hips will make the area appear wider and more curvy. Be sure to keep the waist in view so you don't add visual weight to your body. A long shoulder bag worn diagonally across your body also will add volume to the hip area.

Step 2 - Adjust the Proportions

Visually widen the hips by narrowing the appearance of your shoulders.

Narrow the shoulders by choosing tops in medium to dark solid colors that emphasize the centerline of the body. Choose halter styles and styles with deep V- or scoop necklines. Details along these necklines will further de-emphasize your shoulders. Tops without collars or with "cold" shoulders or one shoulder also work well.

Skip puffy sleeves, shoulder pads, tube-tops, horizontal stripes, boat necks, square necklines or anything else that makes your shoulders bigger or creates a horizontal line across your torso.

Step 3 - Distract Attention from the Hips

Move the attention away from your hips to your face, shoulders, cleavage, waist and centerline of the body. Choose clothing and accessories with details in these areas to bring the eye away from the hips.

Low necklines, small stud earrings, long pendant and lariat-style necklaces, belts at the waist, bracelets, rings, shoes, long scarves, clutch bags and handbags all work well.

Avoid accessories that emphasize the shoulders, such as dangling earrings, shoulder bags and backpacks.

TOPS:

Note: Tops should be darker than bottoms.

Top with
Flare at Hips

Jacket/Top
with Peplum

V-Neckline

Ruffle Pockets
at Hips

Bare
Shoulder

"Cold" Shoulder

Halter
Neckline

V-Neck with No
Collar or Lapels

Top with
One-shoulder

Asymmetrical
Shoulders

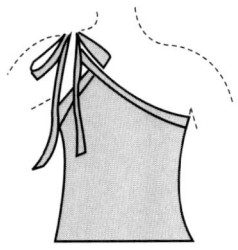

One-Shoulder

BOTTOMS:

Full Skirt

Tiered Skirt

Skirt with Big
Details at Hip

Layered Skirt

Cuff Short-Shorts with
Big Details at Hips

Bubble Skirt

Skirt with Flounce/
Pleats at Hem

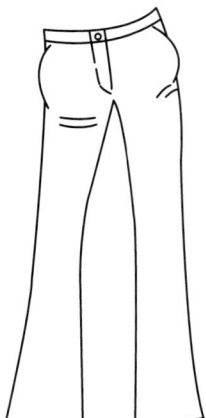

Pants with
Side Seam
Pockets

Pants with Small
Back Pockets

Pants with Flap
Back Pockets

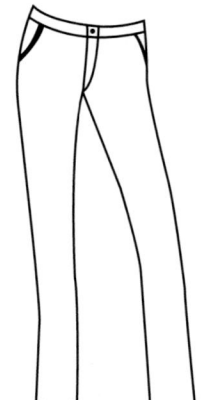

Cigarette/Skinny Pants

DRESSES:

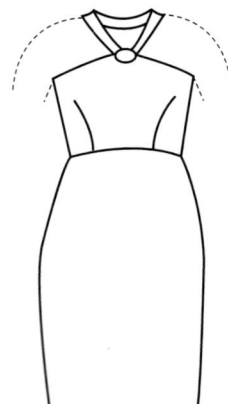

Dress with
Bare Shoulder

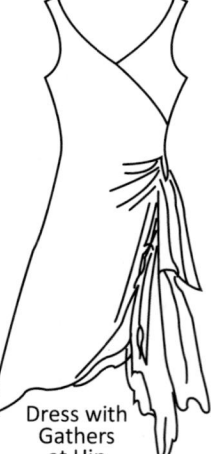

Dress with
Gathers
at Hip

Dress with
Full Skirt

Mock Halter
Dress

Dress with Puffy Skirt

ACCESSORIES:

Note: See chapter 5 for shoe styles and hairstyles.

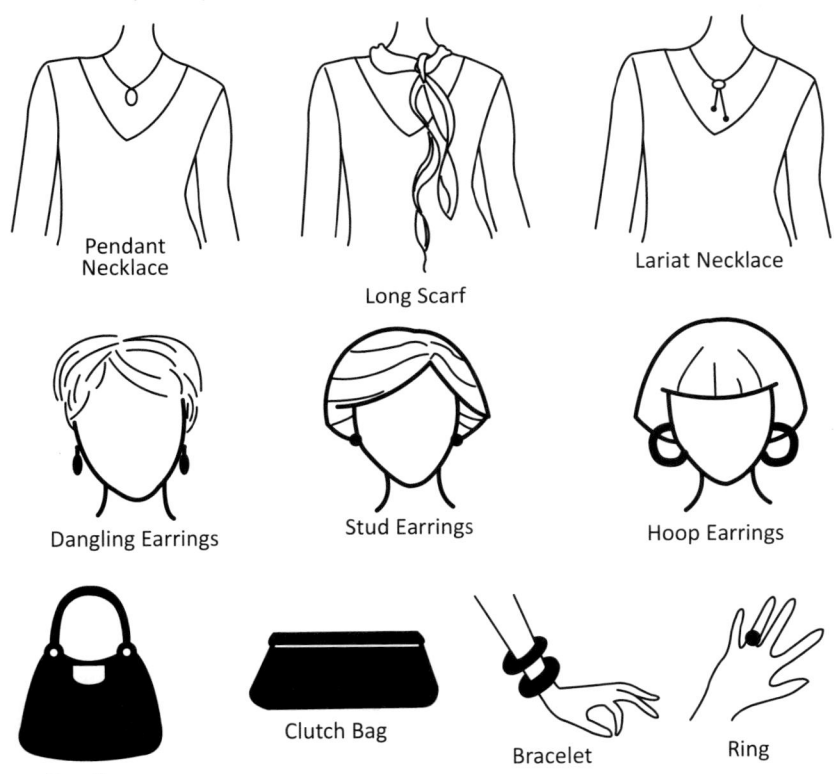

Pendant
Necklace

Long Scarf

Lariat Necklace

Dangling Earrings

Stud Earrings

Hoop Earrings

Clutch Bag

Bracelet

Ring

Handbag

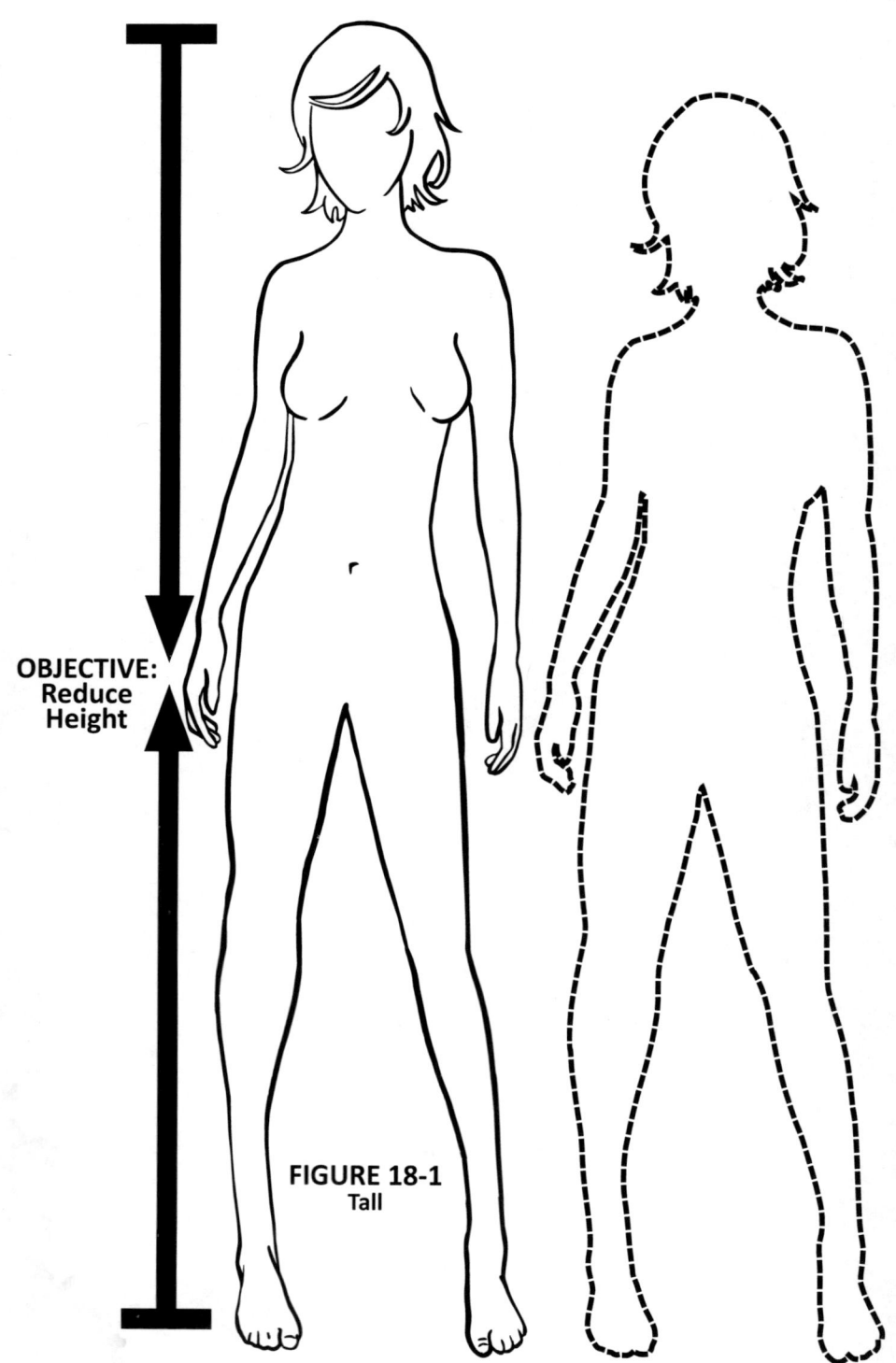

OBJECTIVE:
Reduce
Height

FIGURE 18-1
Tall

CHAPTER 18
Tall

Ellie is a tall woman. She always is on trend and follows the expert advice found in fashion magazines. Most mass-media fashion and style advice is designed to make you look taller, so it doesn't work for her. To shorten the appearance of your height, do the opposite of the recommendations in Chapters 5 and 6. Here are the steps for you.

Step 1 – Maximize Horizontal Lines
Each time you cross the body with a horizontal line, you visually decrease your height by about an inch.

Create horizontal lines by choosing and combining any of the following:

- Tops and bottoms in contrasting colors or shades.

- Horizontal details, such as contrasting stitching, ruffles, pleats and appliqués.

- Fabrics with horizontal stripes or patterns.

- Short necklines, such as jewel, crew or boat necks.

- Boxy jackets and tops.

- Contrasting belts at the waist or hips.

- Short pants, such as Capri pants, walking shorts or cropped pants.

- Skirts and shoes in a color or shade that's different from your skintone.

- Short scarves in a contrasting color tied at the neck or waist.

- Chokers and rounded necklaces without a pendant.

- Short, wide earrings (buttons, studs, hoops, etc.).

- Shoes with ankle straps, horizontal straps or short chunky heels.

- Hairstyles that are wider than they are long, like flips and bobs.

Step 2 – Adjust the Proportions

Each time you emphasize a vertical line or create a "V" on your body, you increase your height. Do everything you can to eliminate vertical and diagonal lines.

Avoid V-necks, pinstripes, princess seams, monochromatic outfits, fringe, long necklaces and scarves, pendant necklaces, long dangling earrings shoulder bags and vertical hairstyles.

Step 3 - Distract Attention From Your Height

Distract attention away from the height of your body and toward your face, cleavage, hands, waist or shoes. Choose jewelry that jingles or moves; contrasting belts, shoes, handbags and clothing with texture, patterns or interesting details.

TOPS:

Bow-Tie Blouse

Boxy Jacket

Gathered & Blousy Top

Boat Neckline

Jewel Neckline

Short Scoop Neckline

Double Breasted Top/Jacket

Horizontal Details

BOTTOMS:

Slit Skirt

Cuff Short-Shorts with
Big Details at Hips

Layered Skirt

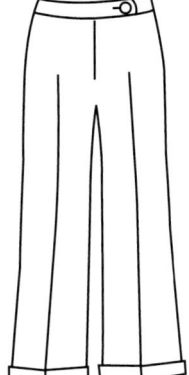

Pants with Cuffs

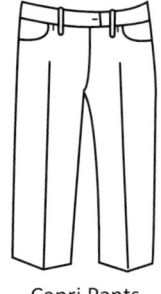

Capri Pants

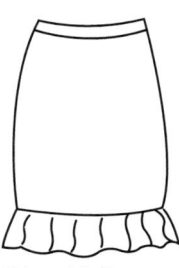

Skirt with Flounce/
Pleats at Hem

Tiered Skirt

Full Skirt

Walking Shorts

DRESSES:

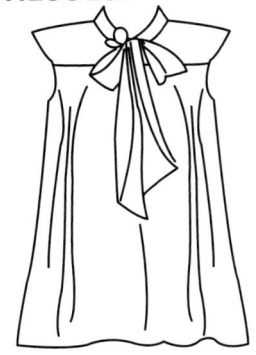

Dress with
Yoke & Bow

Trapeze Dress

HAIRSTYLES:

Bob Hairstyle

Flip Hairstyle

ACCESSORIES:

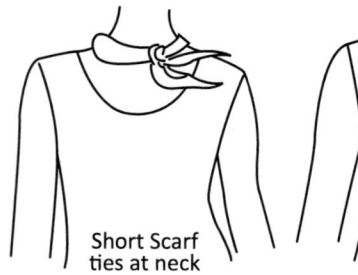
Short Scarf
ties at neck

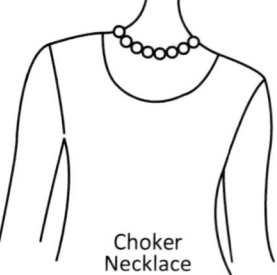
Choker
Necklace

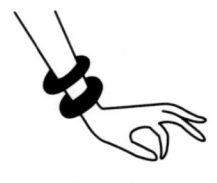
Bracelet

Ring

Hoop Earrings

Stud Earrings

SHOES:

Chunky
Heel

Gladiator
Sandal

High Front
Mule

Shoes with
Ankle Strap

Ankle Boot

Flat Shoe

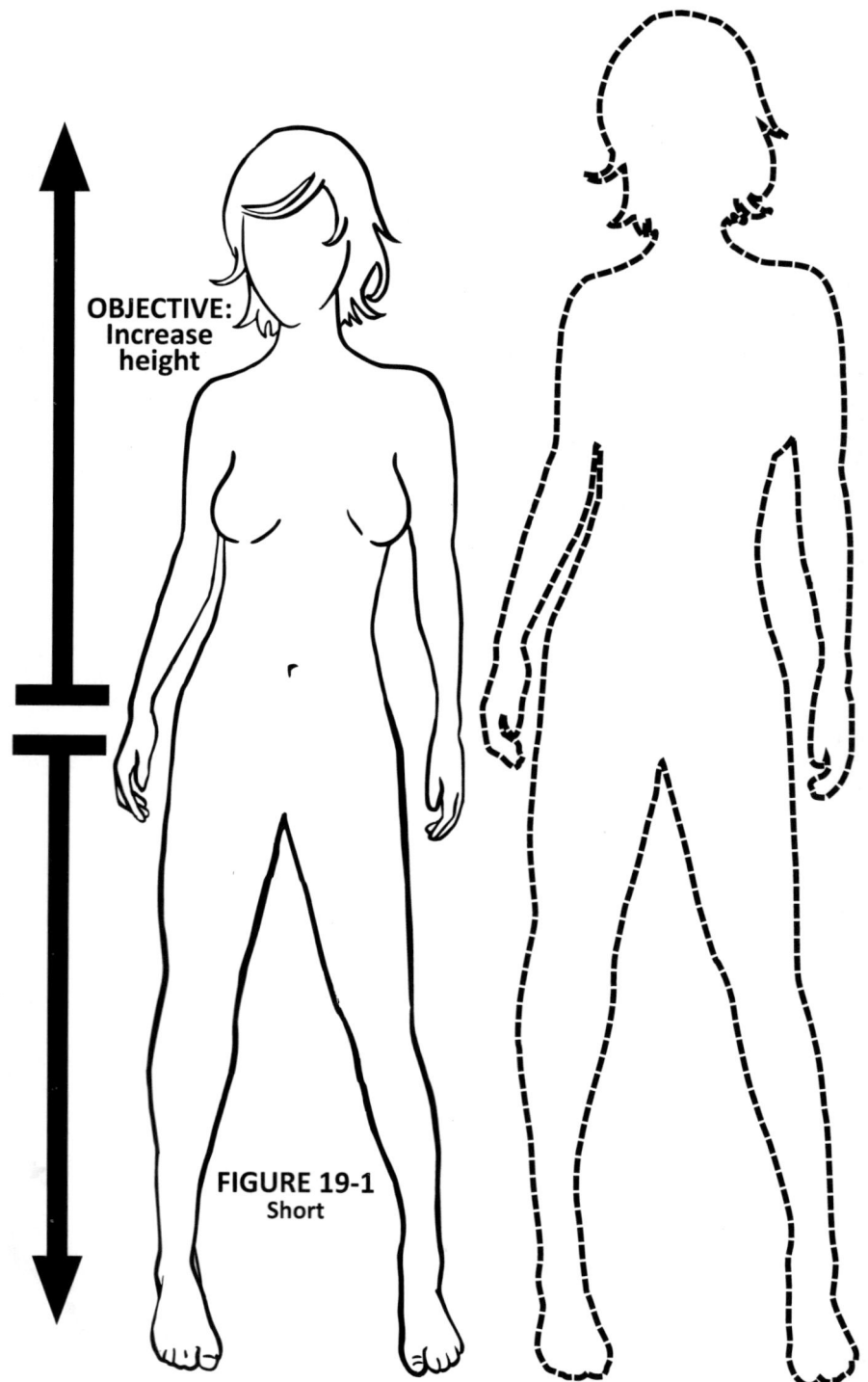

OBJECTIVE:
Increase
height

FIGURE 19-1
Short

CHAPTER 19

Short

Sally is petite, under 5'4" in height. She wears boxy jackets and cropped pants because these are the styles that are most common in the petite department of her local stores. Unfortunately, these styles make her look even shorter. Taking a little extra time to find the right styles or have your clothing tailored to fit you will make all the difference. Here's what to look for.

Step 1 – Maximize Vertical Lines and V's

Each time you create a "V" with your clothing and accessories, you increase your height by about one inch. To increase the appearance of your height, we'll build on the recommendations in Chapter 2 and further emphasize vertical lines and create as many V's as possible.

Create vertical lines and V's by choosing and combining any of the following:

- Tops and bottoms in similar colors or shades. For example, create a monochromatic look all with the same color or create a monotone look from colors with a similar darkness/lightness.

- Fabrics with vertical or diagonal stripes or patterns.

- Deep necklines, such as sweetheart, scoop or deep V-necks.

- Vertical details, such as princess seams, fringe and contrasting stitching or ruffles, pleats and appliqués.

- Garments with V's in the details, such as V-necks, lapels, stripes turned at 45 degree angles meeting at a center seam, jackets with a scallop at the bottom hem and slits in skirts.

- Long, thin scarves tied at the throat or chest with uneven ends.

- Long pendant or lariat necklaces and long, thin, dangling earrings.

- Capri pants, walking shorts or skirts in a shade that's similar to your skin tone. Wear them with bare legs and shoes in a color similar to your skin tone.

- Long pants with the hem about ¾-inch above the floor.

- Skirts hemmed above the knee or no longer than 1-inch below the knee.

- Long shoulder bag worn across the body.

- Pumps, wedges or shoes with platform soles and high heels. Avoid ankle straps or short, chunky heels.

- Hairstyles that are tall, such as up-dos, ponytails and loose, long hair.

Step 2- Adjust the Proportions

Avoid horizontal lines at all costs! Skip boxy jackets, short pants, choker necklaces, short scarves tied at the neck and belts. Beware of horizontal details, such as contrast stitching, piping, pockets and wide or flippy hairstyles.

Step 3 - Distract Attention from your Height

Move the attention away from the height of your body and toward the face, cleavage, hands, waist or shoes. Choose low necklines; dangling jewelry; embellished shoes, handbags and clothing with texture, patterns or interesting details.

TOPS:

Vertical
Pin Stripes

Empire
Waist

Empire Waist Top

V-Neckline

Princess Seams

Scoop Neckline

Create
Multiple "V's"

Diagonal
Stripes

Jacket
with Lapels

Vertical Details

BOTTOMS:

Skirt with Flounce/
Pleats at Hem

Pencil Skirt

Short Skirt
(Hem at or
Above Knee)

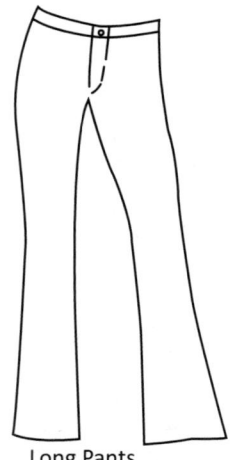

Long Pants

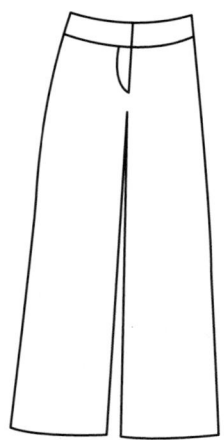

Flat Front Trousers

HAIRSTYLES:

Long Hairstyle

Half Up, Half Down Hairstyle

High Ponytail Hairstyle

Up-Do Hairstyle

ACCESSORIES:

Lariat Necklace

Pendant Necklace

Long Scarf

Clutch Bag

Handbag

Ring

Bracelet

Dangling Earrings

Shoulder Bag Worn
Across Body

SHOES:

Open-Toe Wedge

Flat Shoe

Thong with
Wedge Heel

Open-Toe Pump

Wedge Heel Mule

High Heel Mule

Platform Pump

Kitten Heel Mule

Knee Boot

Closed-Toe Mule

Sling Back Sandal

Pump

Open-Toe Platform
Sling Back

Closed-Toe
Sling Back

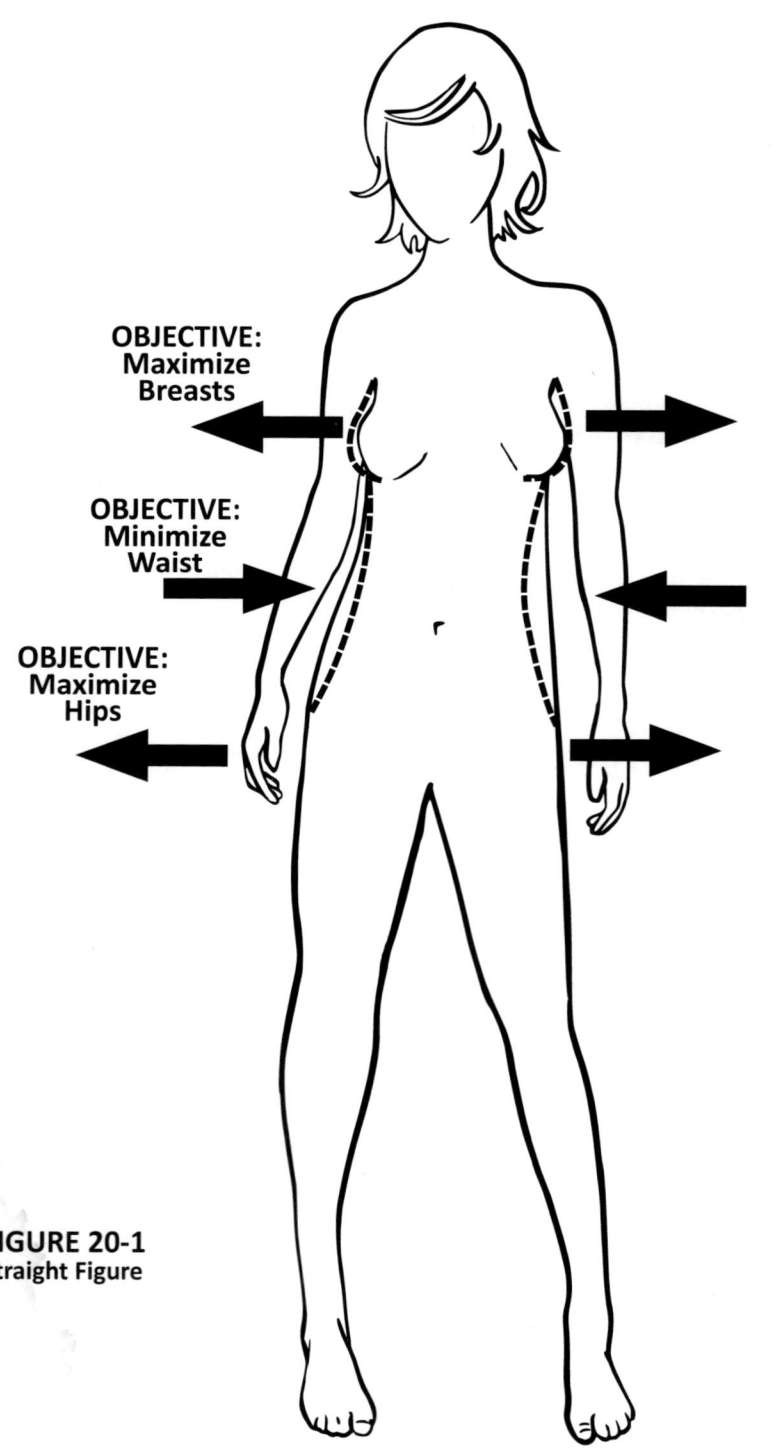

OBJECTIVE:
Maximize
Breasts

OBJECTIVE:
Minimize
Waist

OBJECTIVE:
Maximize
Hips

FIGURE 20-1
Straight Figure

CHAPTER 20
Straight Figure

Lucy has a straight-figure. She wears straight clothing like pencil skirts, shirt dresses and slim-fit pants to emphasize her slim figure. This approach doesn't work because it hides the curves she does have and makes her look straighter than she really is. Here are the steps to give you the illusion of feminine curves.

Step 1 - Maximize the Curves
Maximize your curves by widening the shoulders and hips and adding volume to the bust area.

A great fitting bra will differentiate your bust and your waistline, making the breasts look bigger. Maximizer bras, such as push-up and padded styles, also will add volume to the bust and create even more curves. Tips for getting a great fitting bra are provided in Chapter 3.

Add volume to the bust area by choosing tops with cowl necks, breast pockets, ruching, smocking, ruffles, gathers, horizontal stripes, sequins, buttons, fringe or pleats along the neckline and bust area. These details will add physical and visual volume.

Broaden the appearance of the shoulders by choosing tops with puffy sleeves, shoulder pads, epaulettes, batwing sleeves or short sleeves with tabs/cuffs.

Widen the appearance of the hips by wearing bottoms with light colors, bold patterns or horizontal lines. Jackets with flare or peplum at hips also visually widen the hips. Skinny cigarette pants or skirts and dresses with a full skirt, tiers or a flounce or ruffle at the hem also work well. Voluminous details, such as ruching, ruffles, pleats, gathers or side pockets on the hips also will make the hips appear curvier.

Step 2 – Adjust the Proportions

Making your waist appear smaller will make you look curvier.

Choose slim tops that fit smoothly around the ribcage and waist. Surplice, tailored tunics and fitted button-down tops all work great. Also choose ombre fabrics with the lighter color at bust and hips and the darker color at waist. Button your jacket and sweater just below the bust at the narrowest part of the torso to make the waist appear smaller.

Choose flat-front pants and skirts that fit smoothly around the waist and don't add any additional bulk. Opt for belts that are darker than the rest of your clothing and made from a matte material, such as suede or woven and embroidered fabrics.

Avoid belts that are shiny or reflect light or are lighter or brighter than your clothing.

Step 3 – Divert Attention

Divert attention to the top and bottom of your body to distract from your core. Dangling earrings, sparkling or colorful hair accessories, bangles, rings, embellished shoes, embellished or colorful hemlines on dresses and skirts, handbags and clutch bags all work well.

TOPS:

Boat Neckline

Cowl Neckline

Fringe Details
at Neckline

Sequin Details
at Neckline

Tunic

Top with
Horizontal Details

Flutter Sleeves

Puffy Sleeves

Ruffles at
Bustline

Untucked Blouse

Surplice Top

Ombre with Dark
Tones at Waist

Batwing Sleeve
(Sleeve begins at waist)

Horizontal
Stripes

Horizontal Stripes

Blouse with
Tab Cuffs

Button Jacket Just
Below the Bustline

Peplum

Ruffle Pockets

Epaulettes on
Shoulders

Shrug

Flared at Hips

BOTTOMS:

Long Boot
Cut Pants

Pants with Side
Seam Pockets

Cigarette/
Skinny Pants

Flat Front
Trousers

Skirt with Big
Details at Hip

A-Line Skirt

Layered Skirt

Cuff Short-Shorts
with Big Details
at Hips

Skirt with Flounce/
Pleats at Hem

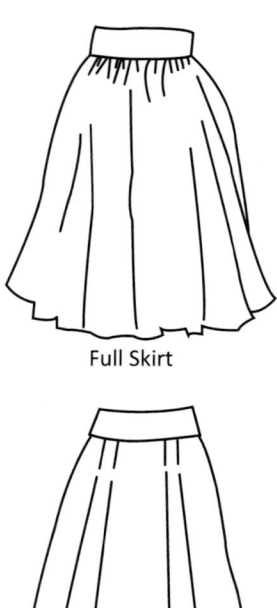

Full Skirt

Bubble Skirt

Tiered Skirt

Skirt with
Box Pleats

DRESSES:

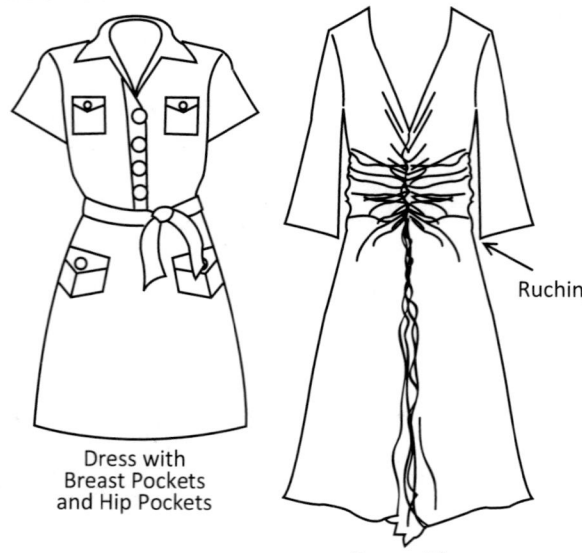

Dress with
Breast Pockets
and Hip Pockets

Ruching

Dress with
Ruching at Waist

ACCESSORIES:

Dangling Earrings

Clutch Bag

Handbag

Bracelet

Ring

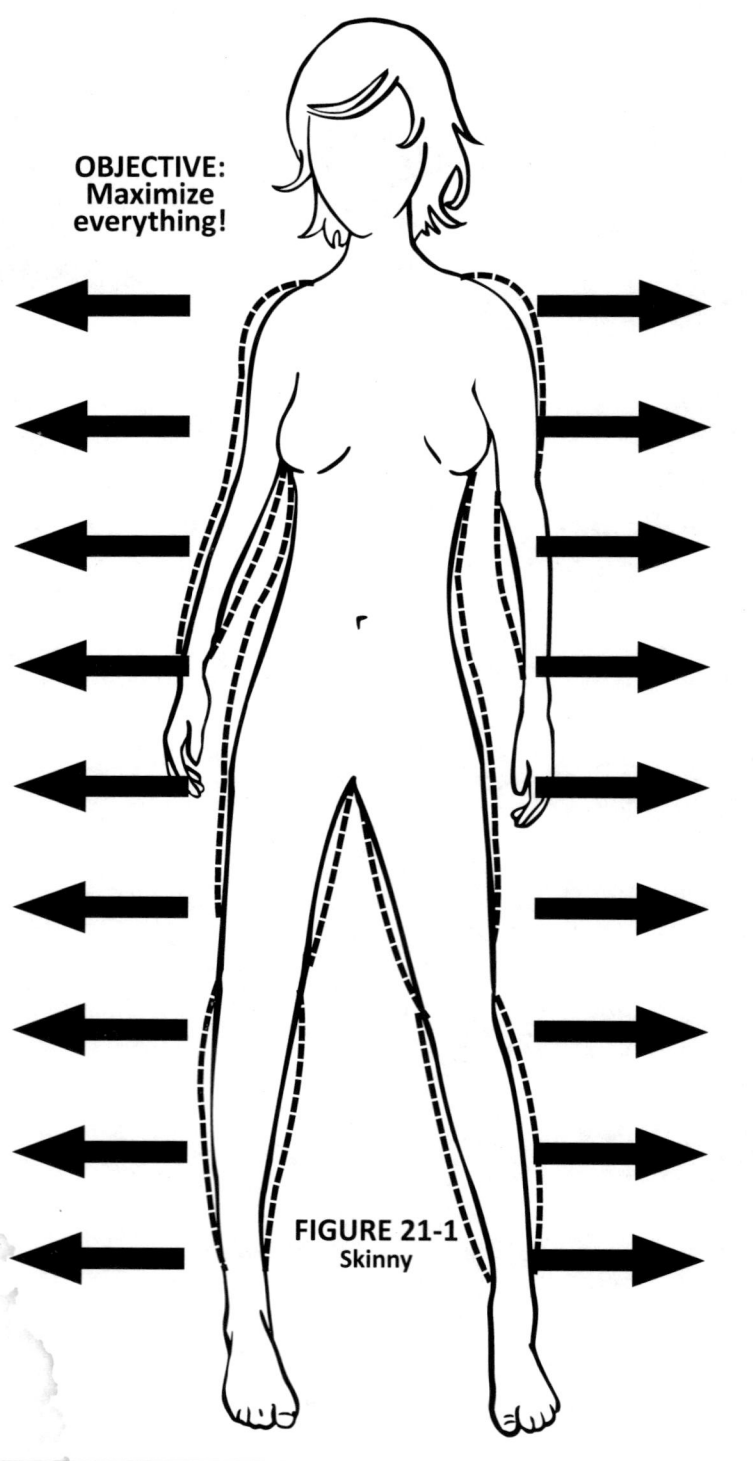

OBJECTIVE:
Maximize
everything!

FIGURE 21-1
Skinny

CHAPTER 21

Skinny

Lily is skinny. She wears her clothing oversized to make her body look fuller. Her garments are so big, she looks like she's floating in the clothes, as if she's playing dress-up in her mother's closet. This approach makes her look smaller than she is. If you're under 30, this approach makes you seem frail and juvenile. If you're over 35, it makes you seem a lot older.

Here are the steps to giving you more volume without sacrificing your figure or strength.

Step 1 - Maintain Your Frame
Choose clothing that fits your body and frame. You can wear big, voluminous and even oversized clothing as long as the shoulders, waist or hips are fitted so the silhouette of your body is partially visible. It's also critical for you to expose some skin on your legs or arms to keep your body from getting swallowed up in your clothes.

Step 2 – Add Volume To Your Frame
You have the ability to wear styles that naturally make you look bigger. You are small enough to wear anything you see on the runway without looking enormous.

You can choose any of these trends and styles:

- Draped and layered clothing.

- Clothing with big gathers, pleats or ruffles.

- Tops and dresses with a yoke and bow.

- Blouses with Victorian collars and pleating.

- Peasant tops and dresses.

- Long tops and jackets with hems that extend below your hipbones.

- Boxy jackets and tops.

- Cropped or swing jackets.

- Shrugs and wraps.

- Trapeze tops and dresses.

- Pants with pleats or gathers at the waist or hips.

- Pants that are tapered at the ankles or skinny pants and pants with cuffs.

- Skirts with voluminous details at the waist and hips, such as bows, ruching, gathers and pleats.

- Skirts that are longer than 2 inches below the knee.

- Bubble skirts.

Step 3 – Divert Attention

Divert attention to the top and bottom of your body with colorful or embellished accessories to distract from your thin core and limbs. Dangling earrings, sparkling hair accessories, necklaces, big rings, colorful shoes, shiny belts, fancy hemlines on dresses and skirts, handbags and clutch bags all work well.

TOPS:

Shrug

Bow-Tie Blouse

Turtleneck

Gathered &
Blousey Top

Boxy Jacket

Long Blazer

Peasant Top

Double Breasted
Jacket/Top

Batwing Sleeve
(Sleeve Begins at Waist)

BOTTOMS:

Layered Skirt

Skirt with Flounce/
Pleats at Hem

Bubble Skirt

Skirt with Big
Details at Hip

Full Skirt

Long Skirt

Capri Pants

Cuff Short-Shorts
with Big Details
at Hips

Biker Shorts

Pants with Cuffs

Cigarette/
Skinny Pants

Leggings

High-Waisted
Tapered Jeans

Pleated
High-Waisted
Pants

DRESSES:

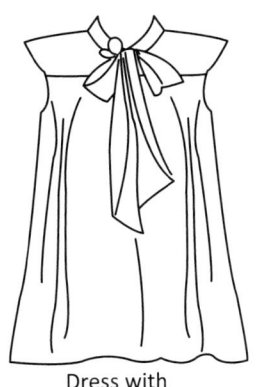

Dress with
Yoke & Bow

Dress with
Volume & Draping

Trapeze Dress

HAIRSTYLES:

Bob Hairstyle

Flip Hairstyle

ACCESSORIES:

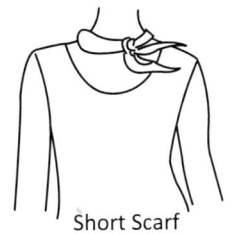

Short Scarf

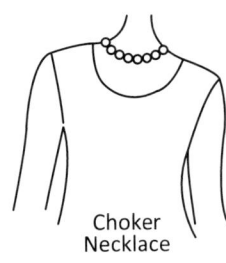

Choker
Necklace

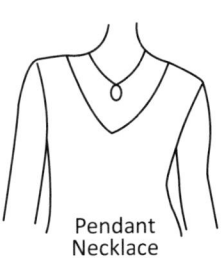

Pendant
Necklace

Lariat
Necklace

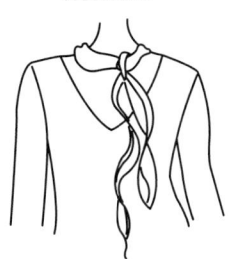

Long Scarf

Ring

Bracelet

Stud Earrings

Hoop Earrings

Dangling Earrings

Long Shoulder Bag

Handbag

SHOES:

Shoe with Ankle Strap

Flat Shoe

Chunky Heels

Gladiator Sandal

CHAPTER 22

Some Final Thoughts

Fashion can be – and should be – fun. Now, with your new found arsenal of dressing and shopping tricks, I hope you'll have more fun in your clothing choices and see the beautiful woman you are appear in the mirror.

"Now that you have completed your transformation, I invite you to take another picture of yourself, as you did at the beginning of our *Dress Yourself Skinny* adventure together. Compare this "after" picture to your previous picture to see how implementation of these tips and strategies makes a difference in your body's appearance.

Reconfirm your body type anytime your weight changes by 15 pounds or any measurement changes by 2 or 3 inches.

To further refine your dressing strategy, you also might look at the opposite body type to yours to see what clothes to avoid. For instance, if you have big breasts, look at the strategy and diagrams for small breasts to see what would make your bust look even fuller. Then you can eliminate these items from your wardrobe and avoid these styles in future shopping trips.

This book contains general information. If several body types apply to you, review the tips and diagrams for both body types and eliminate all conflicting info to create a custom strategy just for you. If you find that a specific tip doesn't work for you, feel free to skip it or post a question at the Dress Yourself Skinny blog at www.DressYourselfSkinny.com.

Finally, it's OK to break the rules and wear any items you want. Now you'll wear them with the knowledge of what you're doing.

Thank you so much for reading!

Please keep in touch on the Dress Yourself Skinny blog and let me know what you tried, what worked, and if you came up with any new Dress Yourself Skinny tricks to share.

GLOSSARY

A

A-line - A dress or skirt silhouette that is narrower at the top, flaring gently wider toward the bottom, resembling the letter A (p. 16).

Ankle boot - A short boot that covers the foot and extends up to the ankle (p. 22).

Ankle strap - A strap or binding on a shoe that wraps around the ankle to hold the heel onto the shoe (p. 22).

Asymmetrical neckline - This neckline appears different on either side of the center front. Necklines with one shoulder strap or off-the-shoulder styles that slip off one shoulder are examples of this type of neckline (p. 41).

B

Backpack – A bag carried on the back with two straps that are looped over the shoulders (p. 60).

Batwing sleeve - A loose, long sleeve shaped like a wing with a large armhole and a tight wrist (p. 20).

Bike shorts – Skin-tight, knee-length shorts made of a stretch fabric (p. 20).

Blazer – A type of single-breasted jacket with patch-pockets and notched lapels. The jacket usually covers the rear end and the length extends to the finger tips when arms are resting at the sides (p. 20).

Boat neckline – A neckline that follows the collarbone from shoulder to shoulder and completely covers the décolleté. Also called a bateau or Sabrina neckline (p. 40).

Bob hairstyle - A short, women's hairstyle where the hair is cut to neck-length all around the head (p. 12).

Body shaper - An elasticized, flexible undergarment worn over the torso, waist and/or hips, to give the body a more smooth and slender appearance (p. 4).

Boot-cut pants – Pants that are fitted in the seat and thigh, tapered to the knee and flared at the ankle (p. 17).

Bow-tie blouse – A loosely fitting blouse with a yoked, high collar and long ties that can be tied in to a soft bow at the neck (p. 20).

Box pleat – A flat pleat made from two small, back-to-back outward facing pleats that have a box-like appearance. Box pleats often are used below the yoke of a blouse or around the waist of a skirt to give a fitted appearance and still allow ease of movement (p. 47).

Boxy jacket – A jacket with straight sides, without definition or curve at the waist (p. 20).

Bubble skirt - A voluminous skirt with a poof at the hem, resembling a balloon (p. 41).

C

Capri pants – Women's pants that are hemmed at -- or just -- below the calf. Some styles also have a slit on the outside of the leg opening (p. 20).

Choker necklace – A necklace that fits tightly around the throat (p. 22).

Closed-toe shoe – Shoe styles that conceal the toes (p. 13).

Clutch bag – A woman's strapless purse that is carried in the hand (p. 17).

Cigarette pants – Slim-fit pants with a snug fit through the legs, ending in a small opening at the ankle. Some styles have zippers or buttons at the leg opening to allow the foot to pass (p. 21).

Cold shoulder – A long-sleeve shirt or blouse where fabric has been cut away to reveal the shoulders (p. 53).

Color block – Large rectangles of color that are printed or sewn on a garment (p. 67).

Cowl neckline - A collar on a woman's top or sweater that drapes in large folds in a scooping fashion around the neck (p. 46).

Cuff – An extra layer of fabric that flips up at the end of a sleeve or pant leg (p. 21).

D

Dangling earrings - Earring style that literally dangle from the earlobe. These earrings are suspended from the ear on posts or wires. Sizes can vary; small ones hang just below the ear while larger ones can be long enough to rest on the shoulders. Also known drop earrings (p. 12).

Demi Bra – A bra that covers the nipples and bottom half of the breasts and leaves the upper part of the breasts and cleavage exposed. Also known as a half bra (p. 4).

Diagonal stripe – A straight, slanted stripe (p. 12).

Double breasted – A jacket or blouse with front panels that overlap and are secured by two separate rows of vertical buttons at the center of the front of the garment (p. 20).

Drop waist - Waistline positioned several inches below natural waist (p. 47).

E

Empire waist - A high waist, positioned just below the bust line with a flowing, loose bodice (p. 65, 67).

Epaulette – A shoulder piece, ornament or decoration often with braiding or other trim for a military or safari-inspired look (p. 58).

F

Flap pocket – A pocket with an overlapping flap that covers access to a pocket. Often, the pocket has a button closure to hold the flap down (p. 21).

Flat-front pants – Pants that lay flat against the body with a flat waistband without belt-loops, pleats, gathers, pockets or any other details that add bulk (p. 16).

Flip hairstyle – A shoulder-length hairstyle that curls up at the bottom (p. 22).

Flounce – A strip of bias-cut fabric formed into a loose ruffle and attached to the hem of a sleeve, blouse or skirt (p. 54).

Flutter sleeves - A short sleeve that fits loosely and drapes in folds over the upper arm (p. 46).

Fringe - A decorative band or edging made of hanging threads, cords, strips or tassels (p. 12, 46).

Full skirt – A wide, voluminous skirt gathered at the waist (p. 41).

G

Gladiator sandal - A sandal with horizontal straps across the top holding the sole to the foot and straps that wind around the ankle or calf. The shoes can vary from flat to high-heel platform soles (p. 22).

H

Halter neckline – A top with shoulder straps that tie behind the neck and across the back, leaving the arms, shoulders and back bare (p. 53).

Handbag – A small bag with a short handle carried in the hand or on the forearm. Also called a purse or pocketbook (p. 17).

High-leg brief - This panty style has a wide leg opening that exposes the thigh and hip, with a full coverage back. Also known as a French Cut brief (p. 4).

High-waist – A garment with a waist line that lies 2 to 3 inches above the natural waist (p. 80, 81).

Horizontal stripe – A straight stripe that goes from left to right (p. 20).

Hoop earring - A circular-shaped earring made from metal wire or tubing (p. 81).

J

Jewel neckline - A high, round neckline that reveals the throat and collar bones. Also called a T-shirt neck (p. 20).

K

Kitten heel – A shoe with a low, dainty, narrow heel, usually about 1-inch high with a slight curve setting the heel in from the edge of the shoe (p. 13).

Knee boot – A boot covering the foot, calf and shin all the way up to the knee (p. 13).

L

Lariat necklace - An open-ended necklace without a clasp. It can be fastened by threading one end of the necklace through the other like a lasso or by tying the ends together in front and letting the tails hang at different lengths in front (p. 12).

Layered skirt – A skirt made with several thicknesses of fabric overlaid to add volume (p. 41).

Leggings – Tight, form pants that extend from the waist to the ankles. They usually are made from stretch fabric (p. 21).

Long scarf – A long strip of fabric worn around the neck, shoulders or head for ornament or protection against the cold (p. 12).

Long, shoulder bag - A purse that can be carried by a strap looped over the shoulder or worn across the body. The strap is long enough for the bag to hang at hip level (p. 18, 42).

Long skirt – A skirt hemmed more than 3 inches below the knee (p. 20).

Low-rise – A skirt or pants with a waist band that sits at least 3 inches below the belly button. Also called low-cut, hipster or hip-huggers (p. 74).

M

Mandarin style – A high-collar jacket or blouse with button or frog closures near the shoulder. This fitted top often is made of shimmering silk, embroidered satin or other sensual fabrics (p. 40).

Minimizer bra - A bra with cups designed to reduce the projection of the breasts, making the breast wider and more rounded (p. 4).

Maximizer bra - A bra that give the illusion of a larger breast size with breast positioning or padding such as push up or padded styles (p. 4).

Mule - A slip-on shoe, without a back or strap around the heel (p. 13).

O
Ombre – Shading where the color is graduated from light to dark. The color effect often is printed or woven into the fabric (p. 66).

Off-the-shoulder - A neckline that sits below the shoulder(s) or drapes over the upper arm(s) (p. 59).

One shoulder – An asymmetrical neckline with one shoulder strap. The neckline cuts diagonally across the chest, from one shoulder to under the other arm (p. 40, 53).

Open toe – Shoe styles that reveal the toes (p. 13).

P
Peasant top – A romantic-style top characterized with a low, gathered, draw-string neckline and free-flowing bodice (p. 46).

Pencil skirt - A skirt with a straight and narrow cut that is form-fitting around the waist and hips, and either has straight sides or curves in slightly at the knees. Generally, the skirt is knee-length or slightly above and made of a more structured fabric like twill, denim, wool or leather. Also called a column or straight skirt (p. 41).

Pendant necklace – A necklace with an ornament hanging from its center (p. 12).

Peplum - A ruffle, flounce or flared extension attached to the waist or bottom of a blouse, bodice or jacket (p. 41).

Platform shoe - A style of shoe, boot or sandal with a sole at least ½-inch thick. The sole often is made of cork, plastic, rubber or wood. Platform shoes also can have a high heel to accommodate the higher height of the sole (p. 13).

Pleat – A fold in the fabric of a garment that is sewn or pressed flat. Pleats add controlled fullness and create a tailored fit (p. 47).

Ponytail – A hairstyle in which the hair is pulled tightly into a band or ribbon at the back of the head into a loose, hanging fall. A high ponytail is tied at the crown of the head, while a low ponytail is tied at the nape of the neck (p. 12).

Princess seam – Long, curved seams sewn into the front and back of a woman's blouse or jacket to add feminine shaping to the garment. The seams run from the shoulder/under arm over the bust and down to the lower hem (p. 12).

Puffy sleeves - A short, full sleeve gathered at the shoulder and at the bottom band or hem (p. 58).

Pump - A heeled shoe with a low-cut front that fully covers the toes, heel and sides of the foot without fastenings or straps (p. 13).

Push-up bra - A bra that lifts the breasts to create cleavage and give the illusion of a larger, fuller bust (p. 4).

R
Ruching – Fabric that has been gathered and sewn in place. Elastic often is added to allow the ruched areas to stretch, fit smoothly against the body and camouflage figure imperfections (p. 46, 67).

Ruffle – A strip of fabric that has been gathered tightly on one side while the other side falls in gentle waves. The strip often is used as decorative trim along hemlines, necklines and sleeves. Several strips often are sewn onto panels of blouses and skirts to create soft, feminine texture (p. 46).

S
Sandal – A light shoe consisting of a sole secured to the foot with straps or thongs (p. 13).

Scoop neckline - A low, U-shaped or rounded neckline that exposes the collar bones and décolleté (p. 12).

Sequin – A thin, shiny metal or plastic disc sewn en masse onto clothing. Sequins reflect light and add shimmer, and are used to decorate clothing and accessories (p. 46).

Shoulder bag – A handbag carried by a strap that is looped over the shoulder (p. 42).

Shrug - A fitted, cropped cardigan with short or long sleeves. The shrug is worn over sleeveless or strapless tops or dresses to cover the arms (p. 58).

Side-seam pocket – Pocket opening that is incorporated into the side seams of a skirt or pants (p. 21).

Side-zip pants – Pants with a zippered opening incorporated into a side seam. The front of the pants lays flat against the body (p. 66).

Sling-back shoe – Shoe with an open back secured to the foot with a strap that wraps around the upper heel, usually with a buckle or elastic panel (p. 13).

Slit skirt - A slim skirt that is fitted from the waist to the hemline with a slit in the front or back to allow for movement (p. 47).

Slouchy boot – A boot with a soft, droopy vamp that is baggy around the calf and ankle (p. 22).

Stance – The point where the top button on a jacket hits the chest. In a high stance, the top button rests on the breastbone. In a low stance, the top button rests on the waist or belly (p. 40).

Stud earring – A round earring that appears to float on the earlobe. The earring is mounted on the end of a post, which penetrates straight through the earlobe (p. 22).

Strapless – A neckline characterized by the absence of sleeves, straps or collar, leaving the throat, shoulders and arms bare. The garment fits snuggly on the torso and is kept in place with boning or no-slip silicone strips sewn inside the bodice (p. 88).

Surplice – A bodice made from two pieces of fabric that overlap each other across the bust line or back. The overlapping fabric can cross above the bust line to create a high, boat neckline or drape loosely to create a deep, sexy V-neckline (p. 66).

T

Tab cuff sleeve – A cuffed or rolled sleeve with a tab sewn inside that wraps around the cuff and secures at the shoulder with the button. The tab and button secures the sleeve and keeps it from unrolling (p. 58).

Thong underwear – A panty with a minimal back that begins as a "V" shape at the waistband and then tapers to a thin strip of fabric by the time it reaches the crotch. This style leaves the cheeks of your buttocks exposed. A thong has more fabric at the back than a G-string (p. 4).

Tiered skirt – A skirt made from strips of fabric that are gathered and sewn together in rows, one above the other. Each fabric strip is longer than the one below, so the volume of the skirt increases with length. Also known as a gypsy skirt or prairie skirt (p. 41).

Trapeze dress - A short dress made of loose fabric falling straight from the shoulders with little shaping. The dress typically is more narrow near the armholes and widens towards the bottom hem. Also called a tent or sack dress (p. 21).

Trousers – Wide-leg pants with a wide, flat waistband. The leg opening can be straight or flare slightly from thigh to ankle. Typically, this style of pants doesn't have front pockets; however, they may have back pockets (p. 16).

Trumpet sleeve – A long sleeve that is set smoothly into the armhole and flares toward the wrist. (p. 65)

Tunic – A hip-length, loose-fitting top. This style usually is simple and slips over the head (p. 40).

Turtleneck – A round, high collar that folds over and fits closely around and covers the neck (p. 119).

U

Up-do - Hairstyle in which most or all of the hair is secured on the back of the head. It can be as simple as a ponytail or bun, or a more complex creation of intertwined twists, braids or curls. Half up-do styles are created by pulling some of the hair up onto the head with bands, ribbons, clips, barrettes or pins while the remaining hair falls freely (p. 12).

V

Vertical stripe – A straight stripe that goes up and down (p. 16).

V-neckline – A neckline that comes to a point in the front, shaped like the letter "V." Short V-necks reveal the breast bone while plunging V-necks may expose the cleavage (p. 16).

W

Walking shorts – Short, tailored pants hemmed about 1 inch above the knee. The upper part of the shorts are styled like tailored dress pants or trousers. Typically, the hem is not cuffed (p. 47).

Wedge – A shoe style where the heel runs under the foot, from the very back of the shoe to the ball of the foot. It is shaped like a wedge or triangle. Wedge heels can be thin and low or thick and high (p. 13).

Wrap dress – A dress with front panels that wrap around the body and overlap in front to close. This style of dress has a deep V-neckline and secures at the side with ties or buttons (p. 42).

Y

Yoke – The tailored part of a blouse or dress that fits about or below the neck and shoulders, from which the rest of the garment hangs. The yoke is fitted to the body, while the bodice can be tailored or fall loosely to cover the torso (p. 21).

INDEX

Sarah Shah's style is entertaining, real and revolutionary. She cuts through the usual fashion and "dress for success" advice and actually shows you how to make your image work. Whether it's business image in a corporate setting, fashion trends for the season or creating the body you want by choosing the right clothes, she makes it work for real women and fashion-conscious men.

For information about booking Sarah for keynotes, workshops, TV appearances or one-on-one coaching, please visit SarahShah.com or contact her directly at (713) 686-8587 or Sarah@SarahShah.com.

QUICK ORDER FORM

When you order *Dress Yourself Skinny*, receive the companion *Dress Yourself Skinny E-Workbook* (list price $9.95) for FREE!

Online Orders: visit http://www.DressYourselfSkinny.com
Email Orders: sarah@sarahshah.com
Fax Orders: Fax this completed form to (713) 686-5109
Phone Orders: Call (713) 686-8587
Have your mailing address and credit card ready.

Date _____ Phone _____

Name _____

Mailing & Billing Address _____

City, State, Zip _____

Email Address (for E-workbook) _____

Number of books _____ X ($24.95 + $4.50 shipping & handling each)

Sales Tax: Please add 8.25% for books shipped to Texas addresses.

Payment Total _____

Payment type ☐ Check ☐ Credit Card (circle) **VISA   MC   DISCOVER   AMEX**

Name on Card _____

Card No. _____ Exp. Date _____ CV Code _____

Signature _____

For more info, please visit
http://www.DressYourselfSkinny.com
or **http://www.SarahShah.com**

Sarah Shah's style is entertaining, real and revolutionary. She cuts through the usual fashion and "dress for success" advice and actually shows you how to make your image work. Whether it's business image in a corporate setting, fashion trends for the season or creating the body you want by choosing the right clothes, she makes it work for real women and fashion-conscious men.

For information about booking Sarah for keynotes, workshops, TV appearances or one-on-one coaching, please visit SarahShah.com or contact her directly at (713) 686-8587 or Sarah@SarahShah.com.

QUICK ORDER FORM

**When you order *Dress Yourself Skinny*, receive the companion
Dress Yourself Skinny E-Workbook (list price $9.95) for FREE!**

Online Orders: visit http://www.DressYourselfSkinny.com
Email Orders: sarah@sarahshah.com
Fax Orders: Fax this completed form to (713) 686-5109
Phone Orders: Call (713) 686-8587
Have your mailing address and credit card ready.

Date _____ Phone _____

Name _____

Mailing & Billing Address _____

City, State, Zip _____

Email Address (for E-workbook) _____

Number of books _____ X ($24.95 + $4.50 shipping & handling each)

Sales Tax: Please add 8.25% for books shipped to Texas addresses.

Payment Total _____

Payment type ☐ Check ☐ Credit Card (circle) **VISA   MC   DISCOVER   AMEX**

Name on Card _____

Card No. _____ Exp. Date _____ CV Code _____

Signature _____

For more info, please visit
http://www.DressYourselfSkinny.com
or **http://www.SarahShah.com**